The Benefits of Colouring Books

Have you often started to doodle or colour in a picture you've found in a newspaper only to become so engrossed that you lose track of time? I know I have. Many people think of colouring books as something to keep the kids occupied, of course, this isn't the case in reality. Colouring, or even 'doodling', is something we adults find very satisfying. Colouring is a great distraction from the everyday stresses of life. It is a therapy that can help generate wellbeing of both mind and body. Colouring in is a form of meditation. It allows us to decompress and helps us to relax. Meditation is not easy for a lot of people but colouring in helps us clear the mind a lot easier and create the same meditative state. You won't need to go outside and sit cross-legged under a tree; you can do it sitting in your armchair at home. Whilst colouring the patterns your mind will focus on the present and not the past. Mandalas such as those with concentric circles and other geometric patterns help us become calmer and deal with any work or personal life stress. Our brain has to work on both logic and creativity as we use the analytical part of our brain when choosing colours and creating patterns within the mandalas. These activities help develop fine coordination and motor skills too, very beneficial for both children and adults. When adults colour, they are taken back to the memories of childhood, those work and tax-free days are rekindled in the mind. Those happy memories also help us feel optimistic about the future. You can even reduce anxiety, something that affects more and more adults. Therapists use colouring books in order to help their patients relax. The creative expression helps them go into a relaxed state, offering a more effective basis on which to receive more therapy. Adult colouring books also offer an alternative and change from the day-to-day routine of work, housework and childcare. They offer a welcome break from our day-to-day thoughts too. Colouring pages also help us rediscover who we are and what makes us tick. It can be the doorway into more creative activities such as drawing, painting or even writing. Our creativity is unleashed as we suppress our daily thoughts, and ideas from the subconscious mind come to the surface, ideas that may have been hidden since we left school as we entered the adult world of work and responsibility.

I have included over forty designs in this book, many of which have been repeated, allowing you more than one opportunity in creating your own colouring designs, and relaxing more in the process.

A.R.Khan

Open Your Mind – Open Your Mind

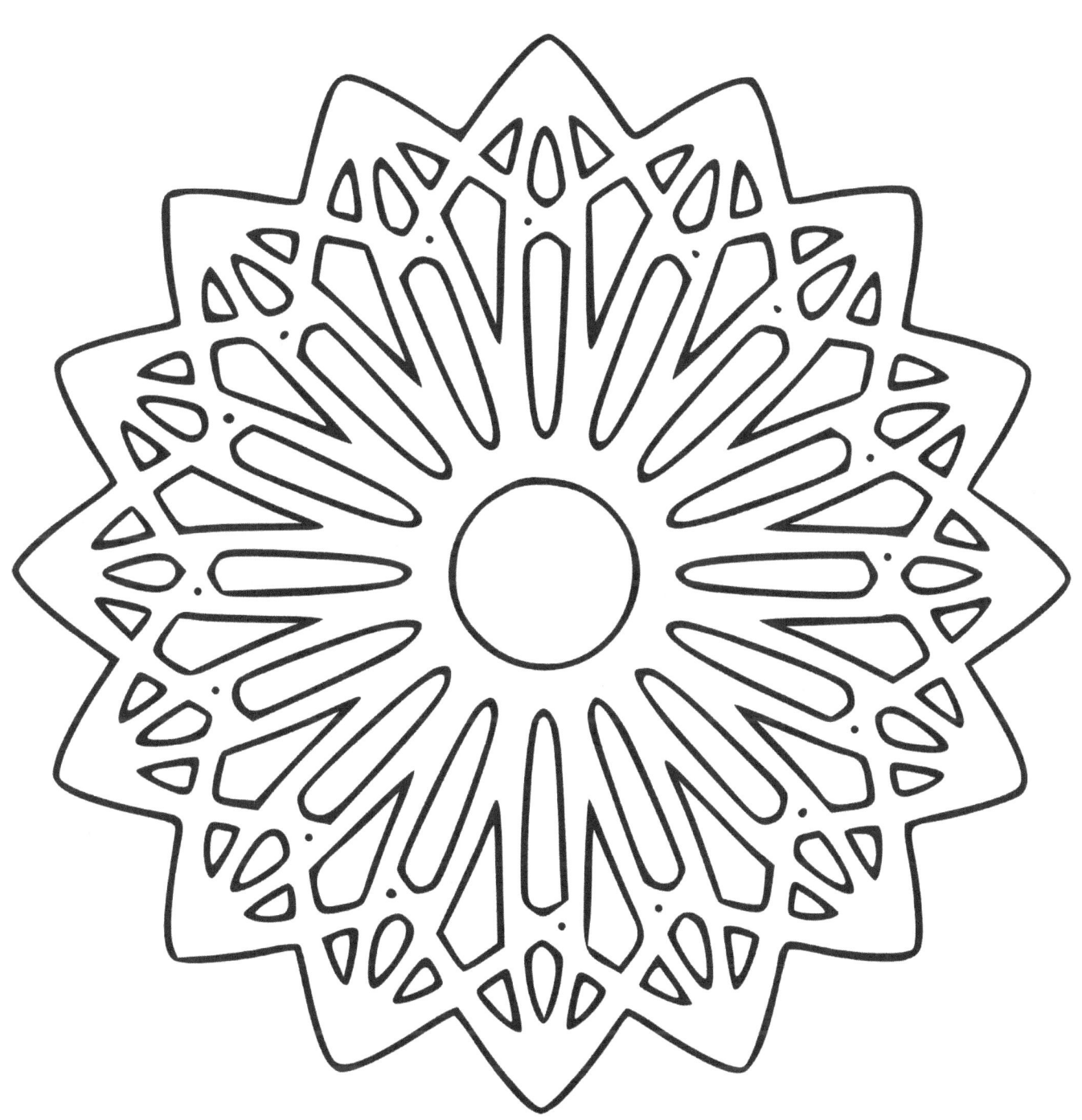

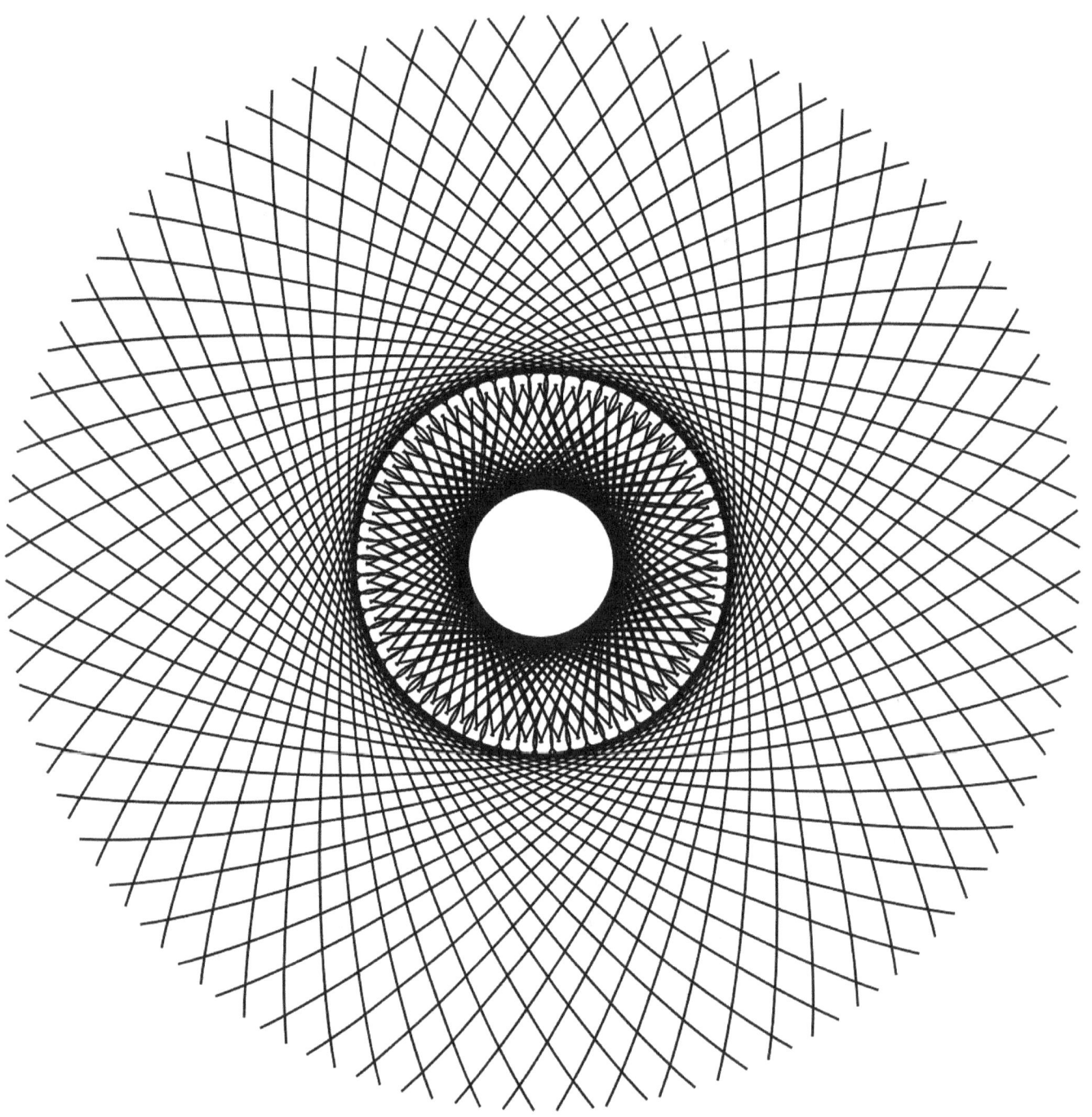

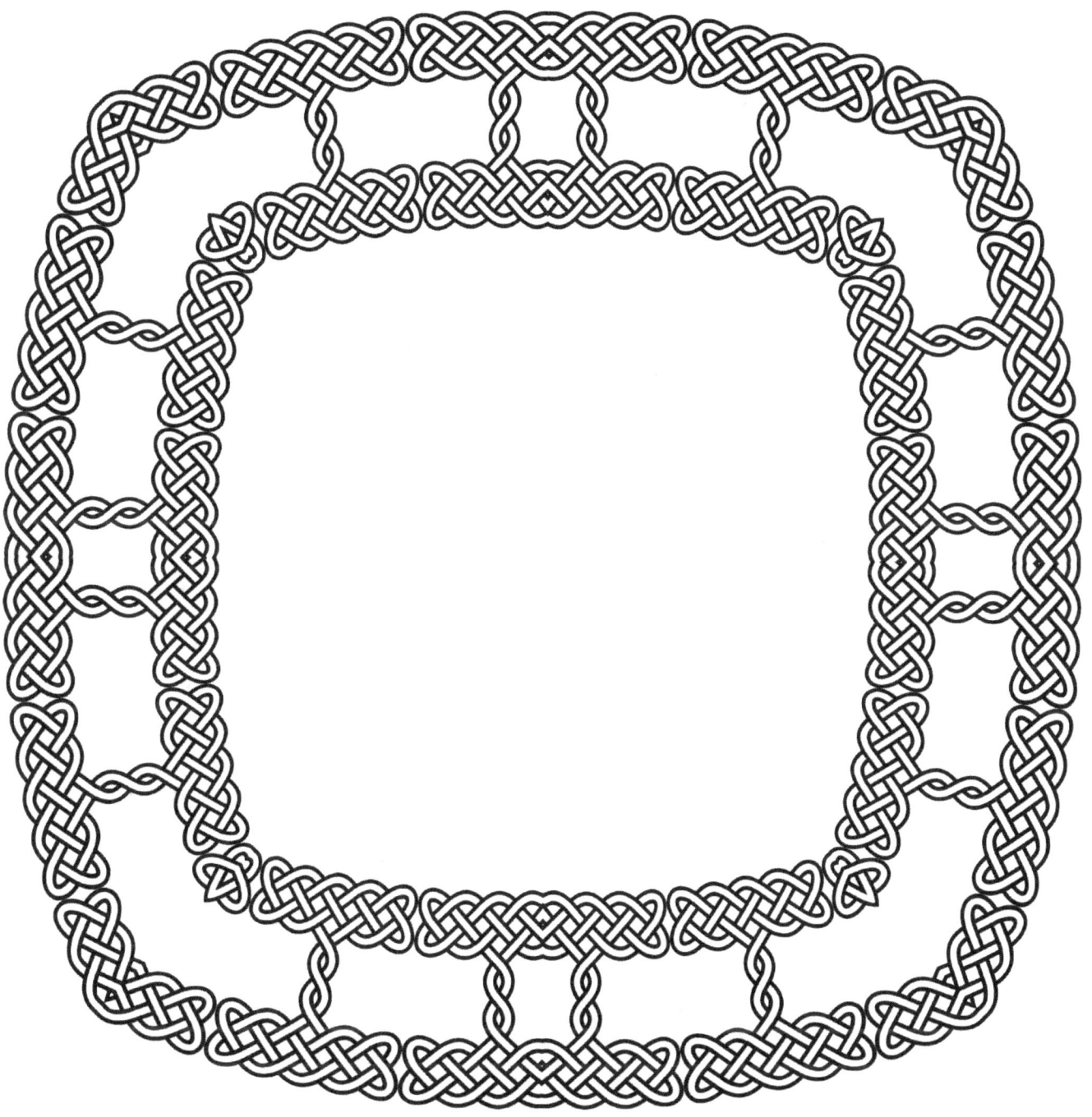

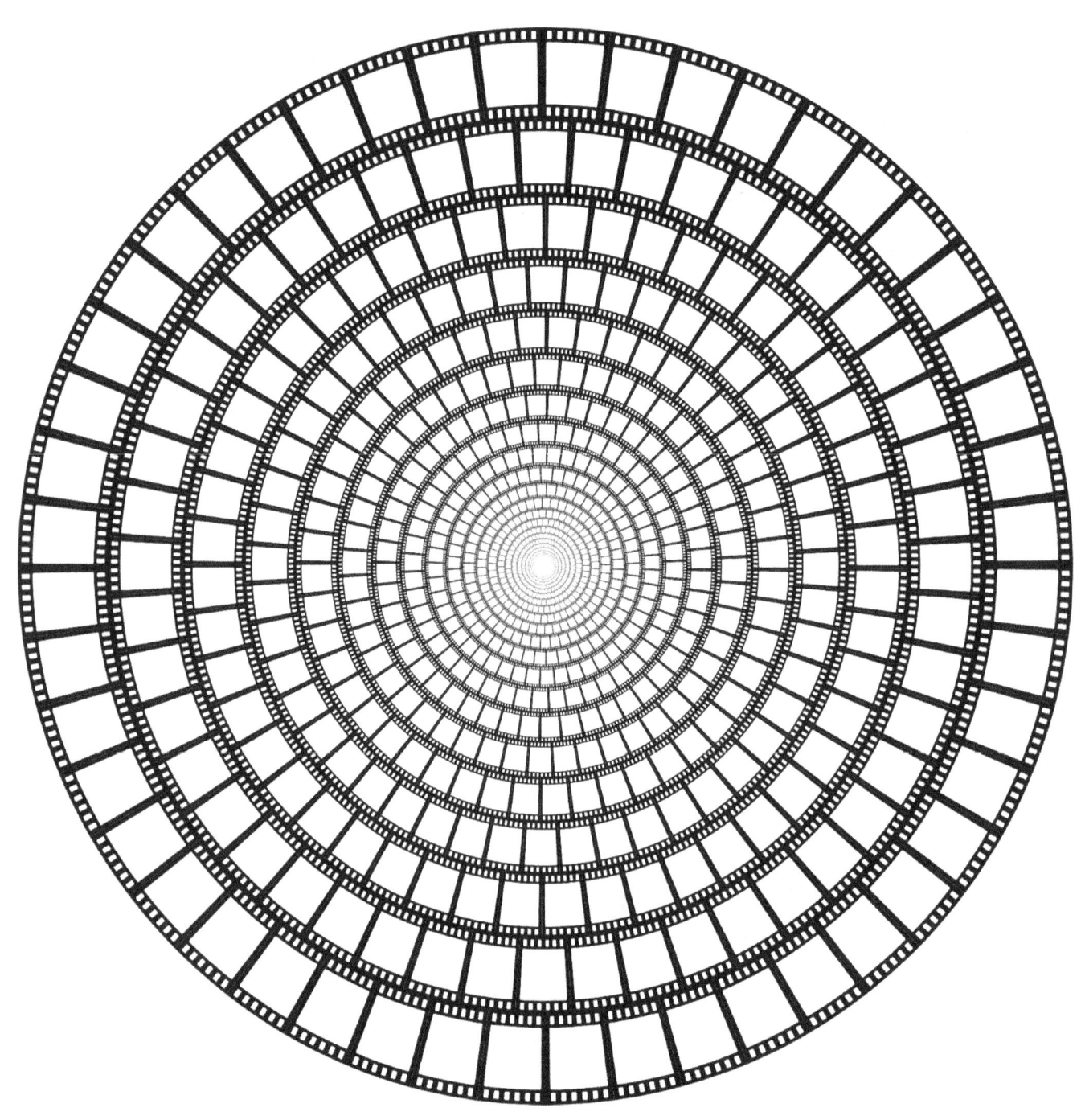

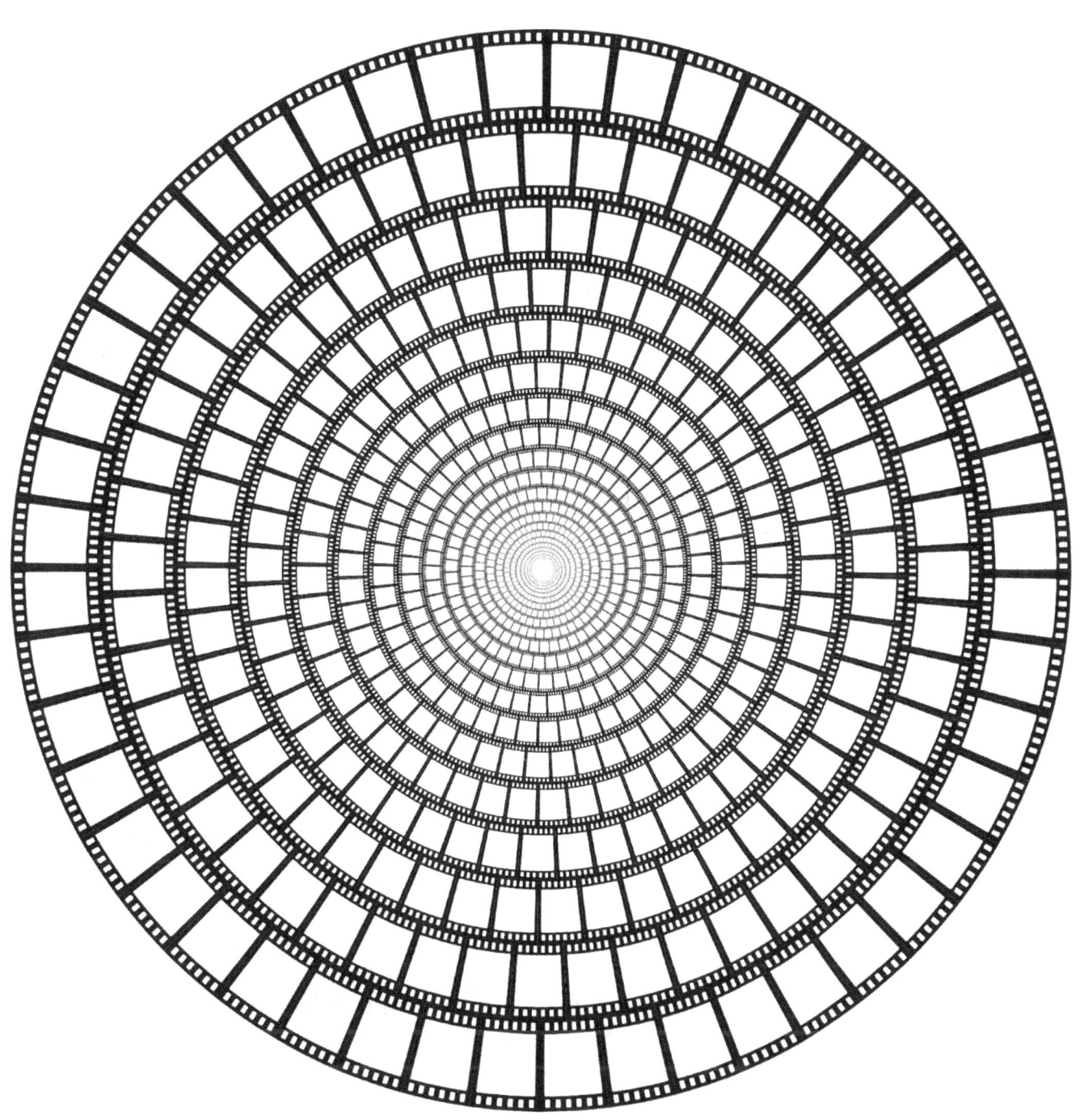

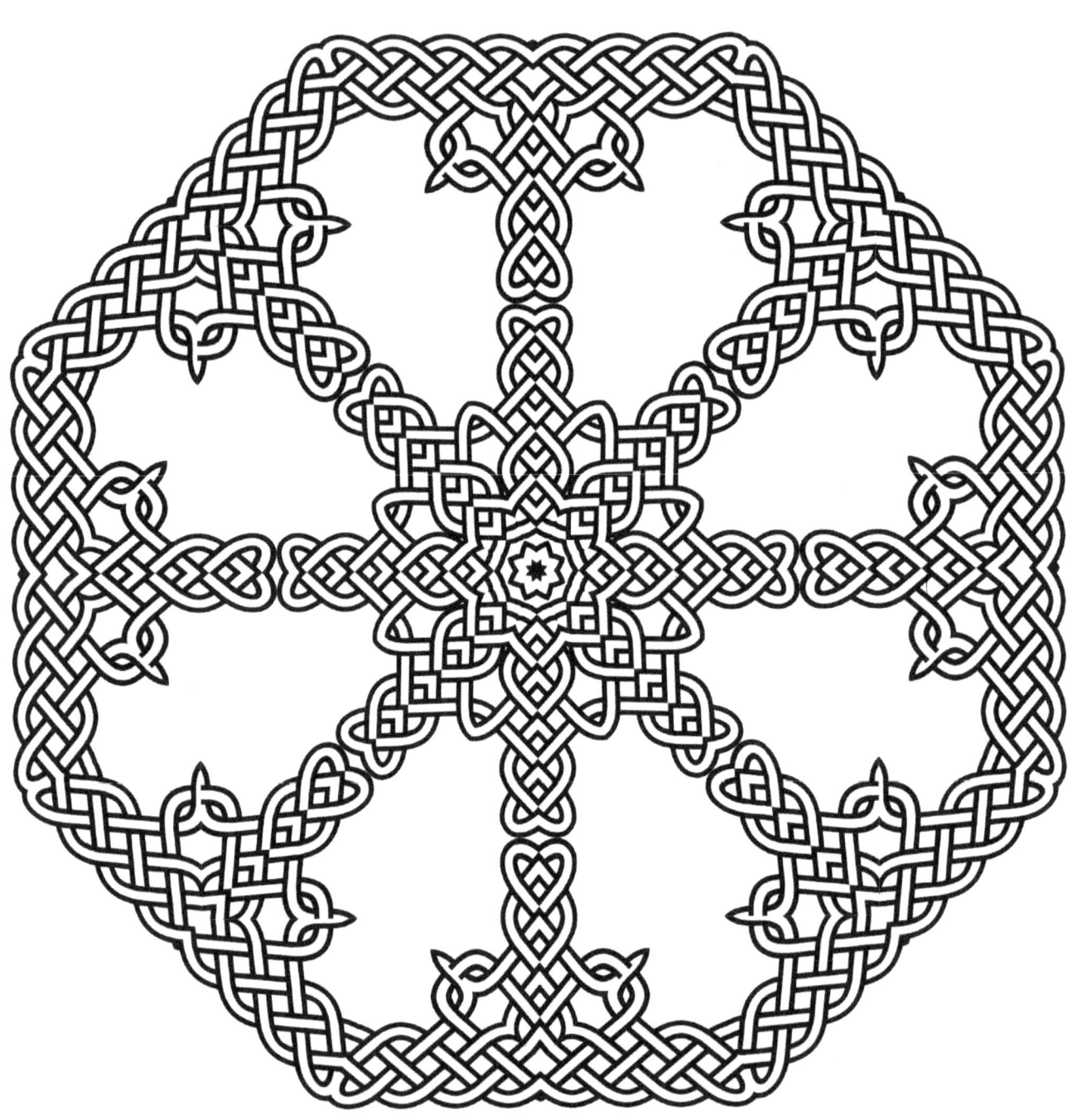

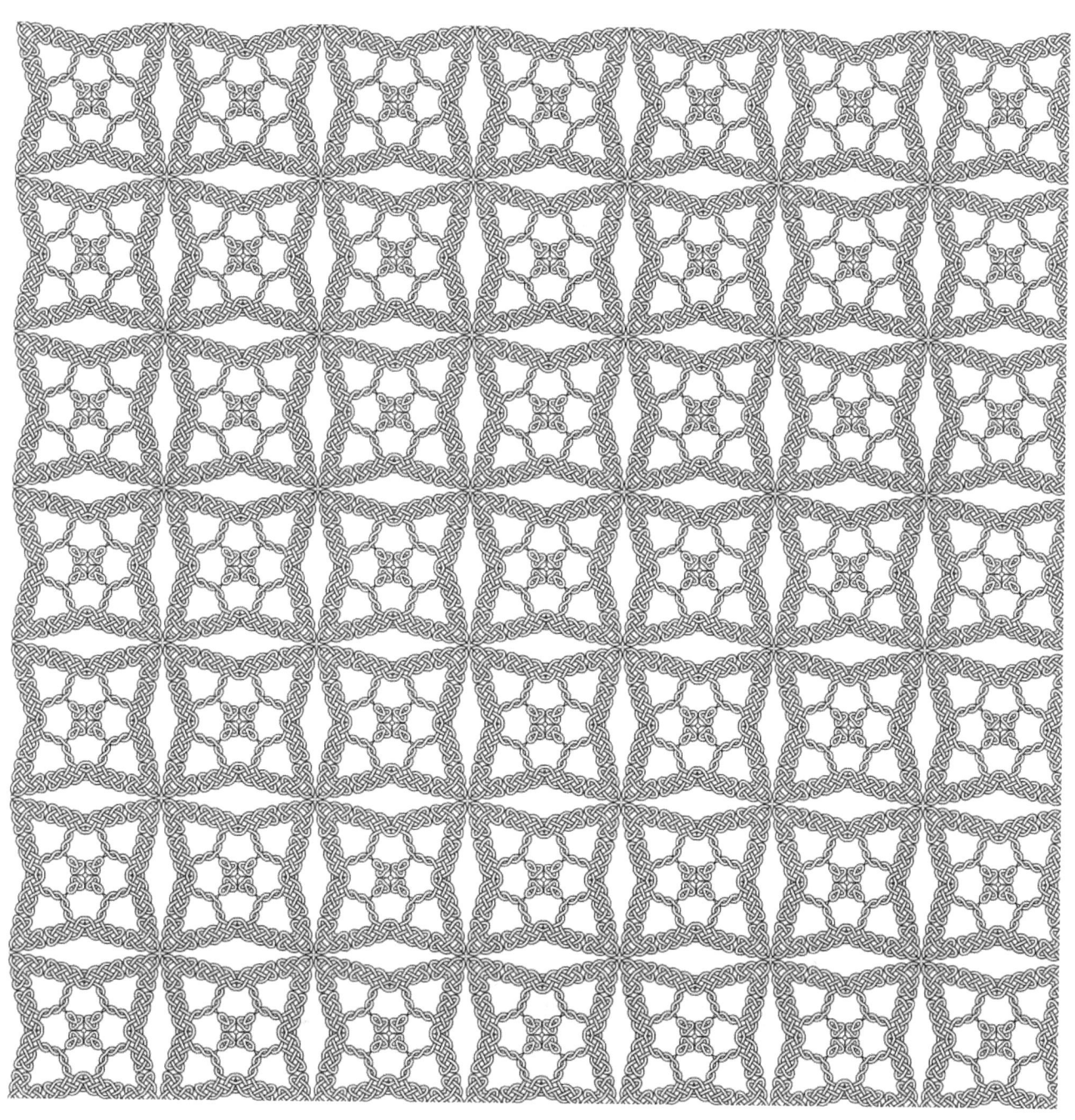

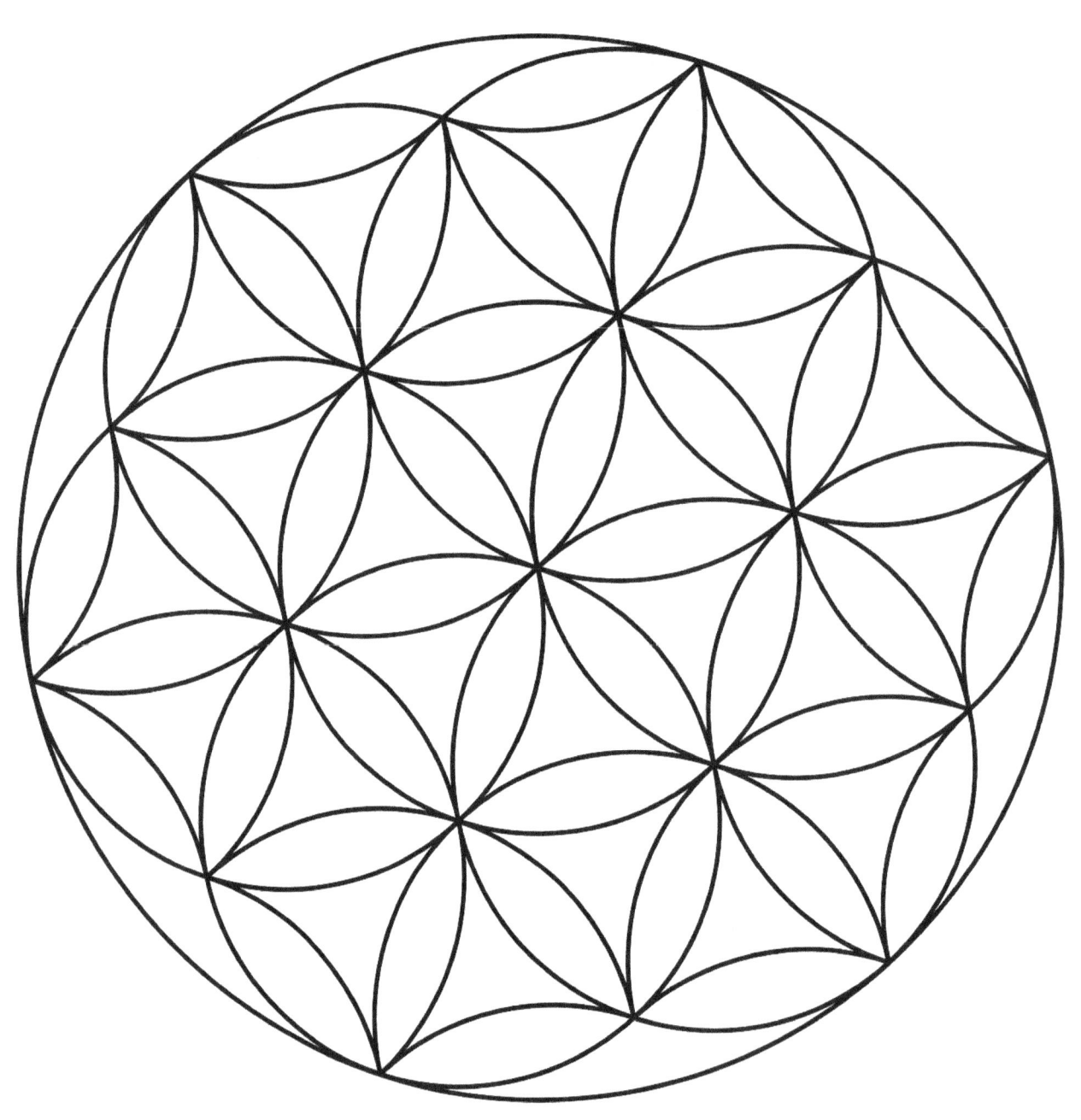

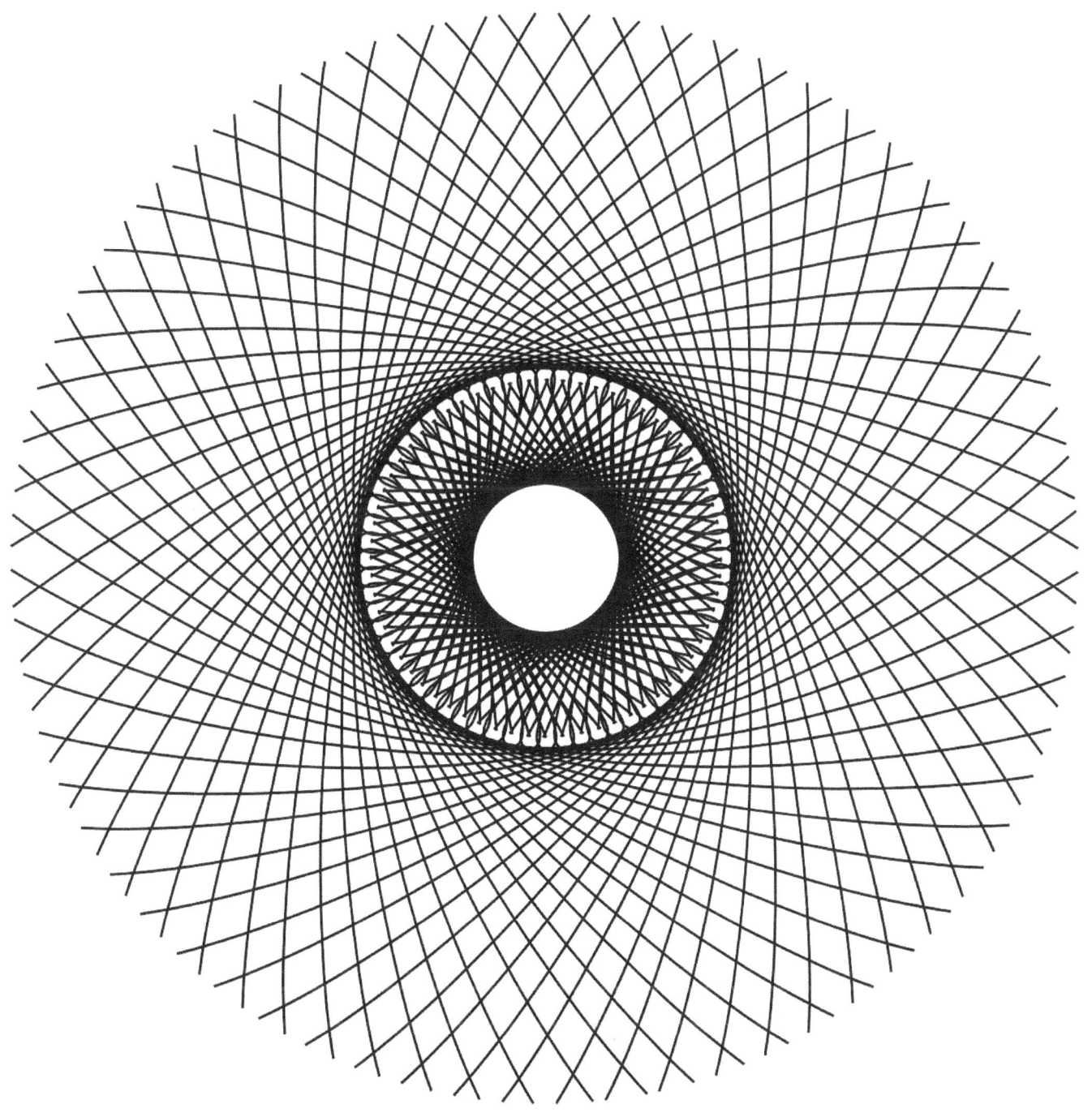

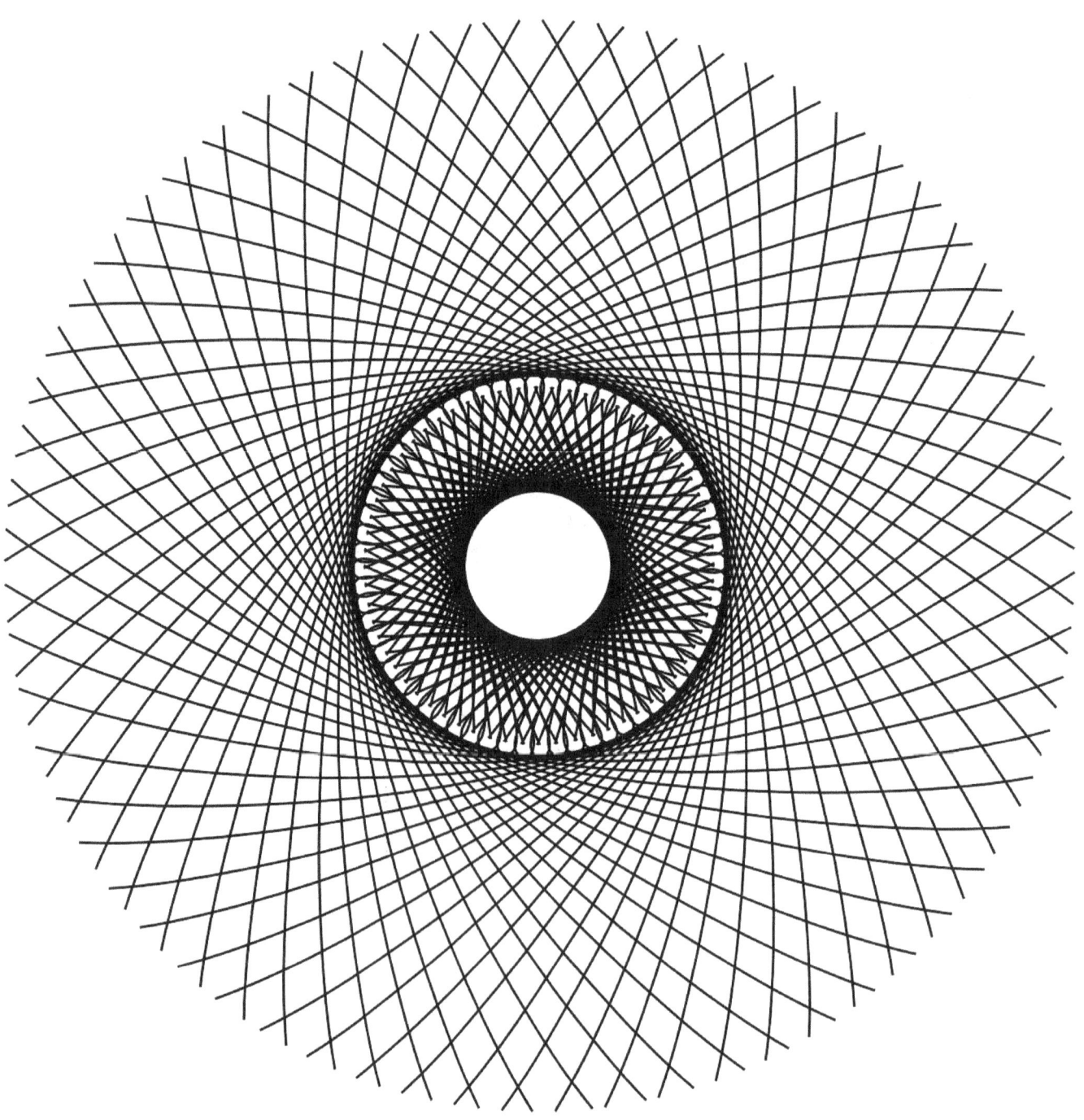

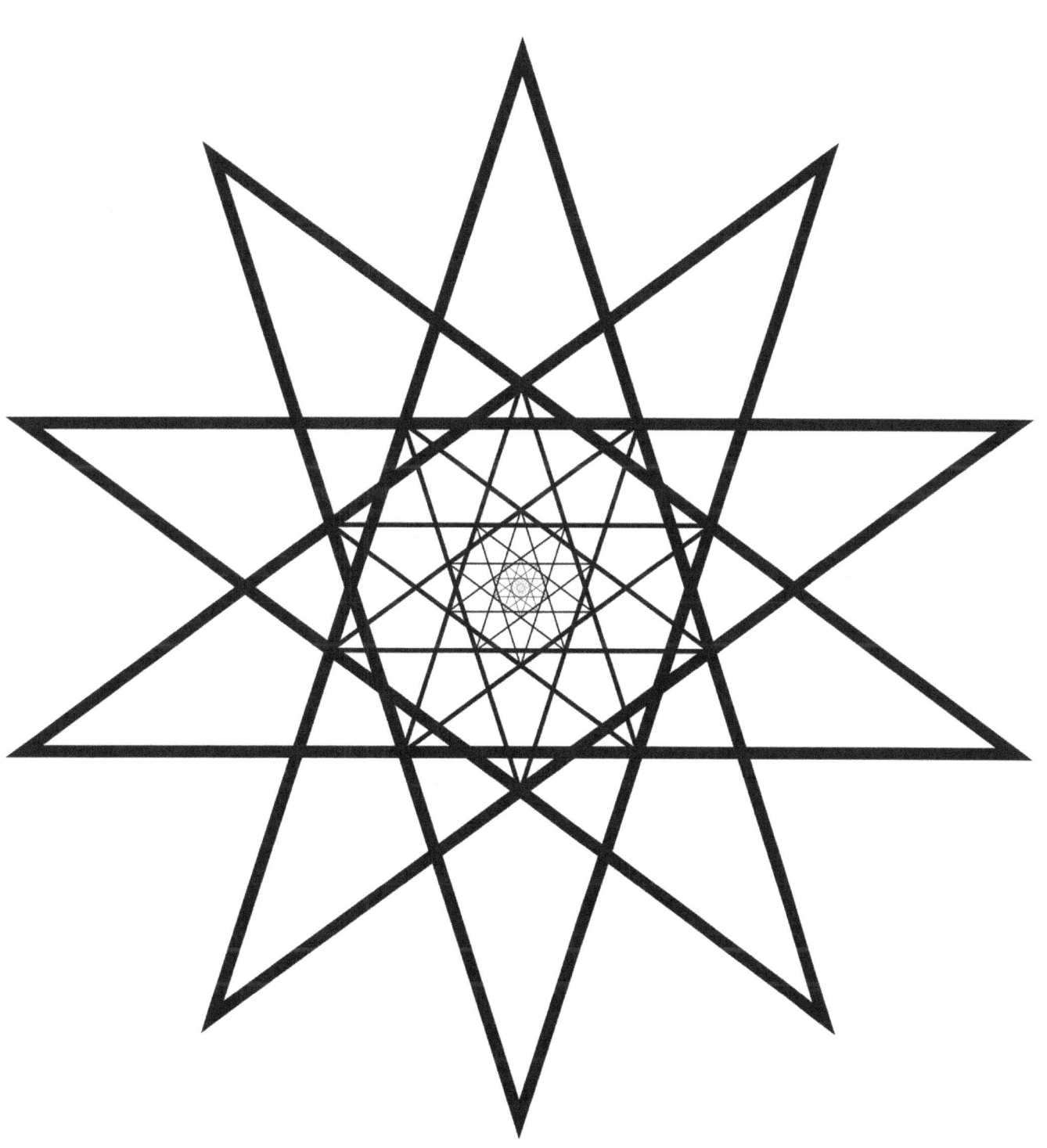

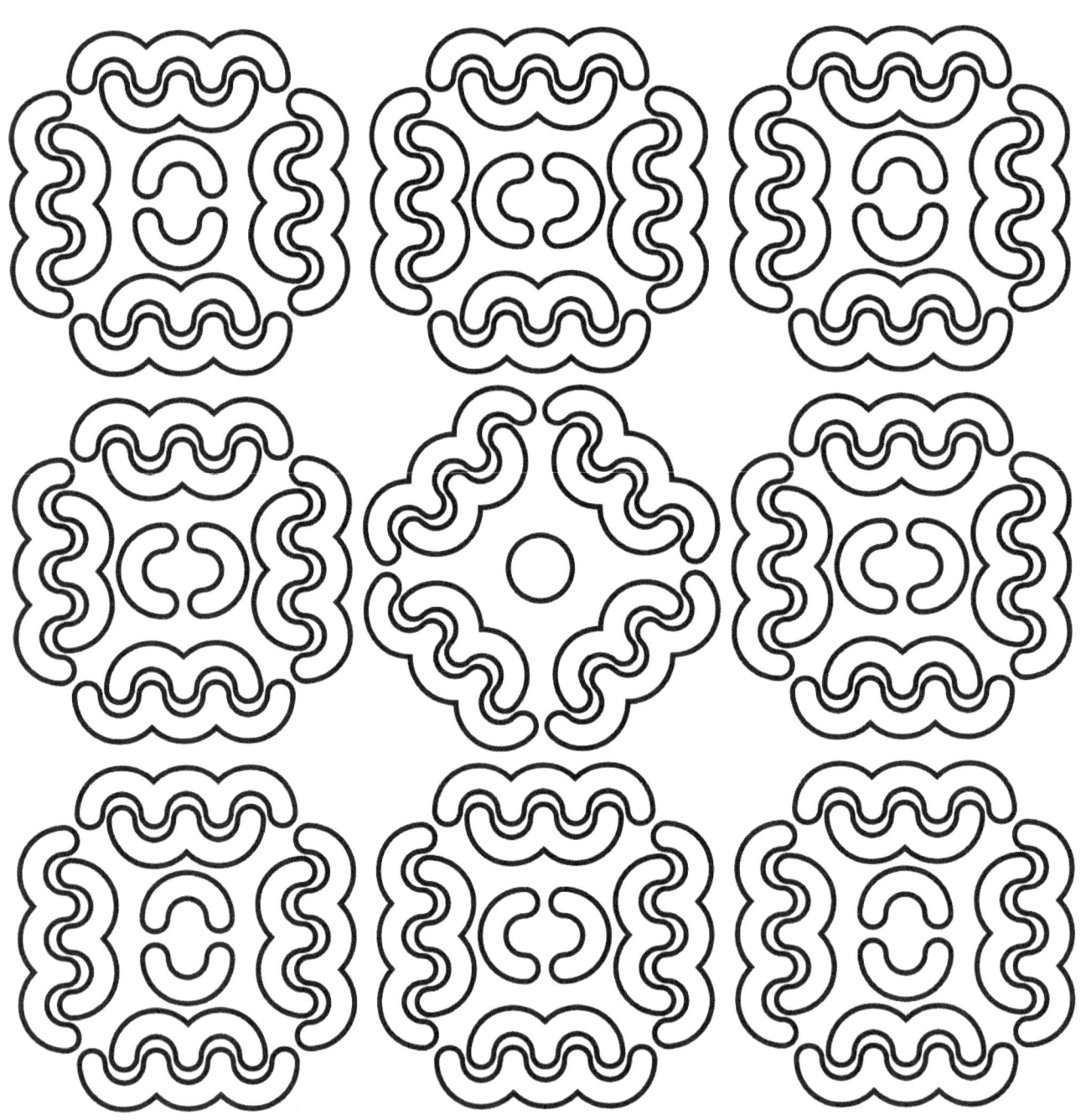

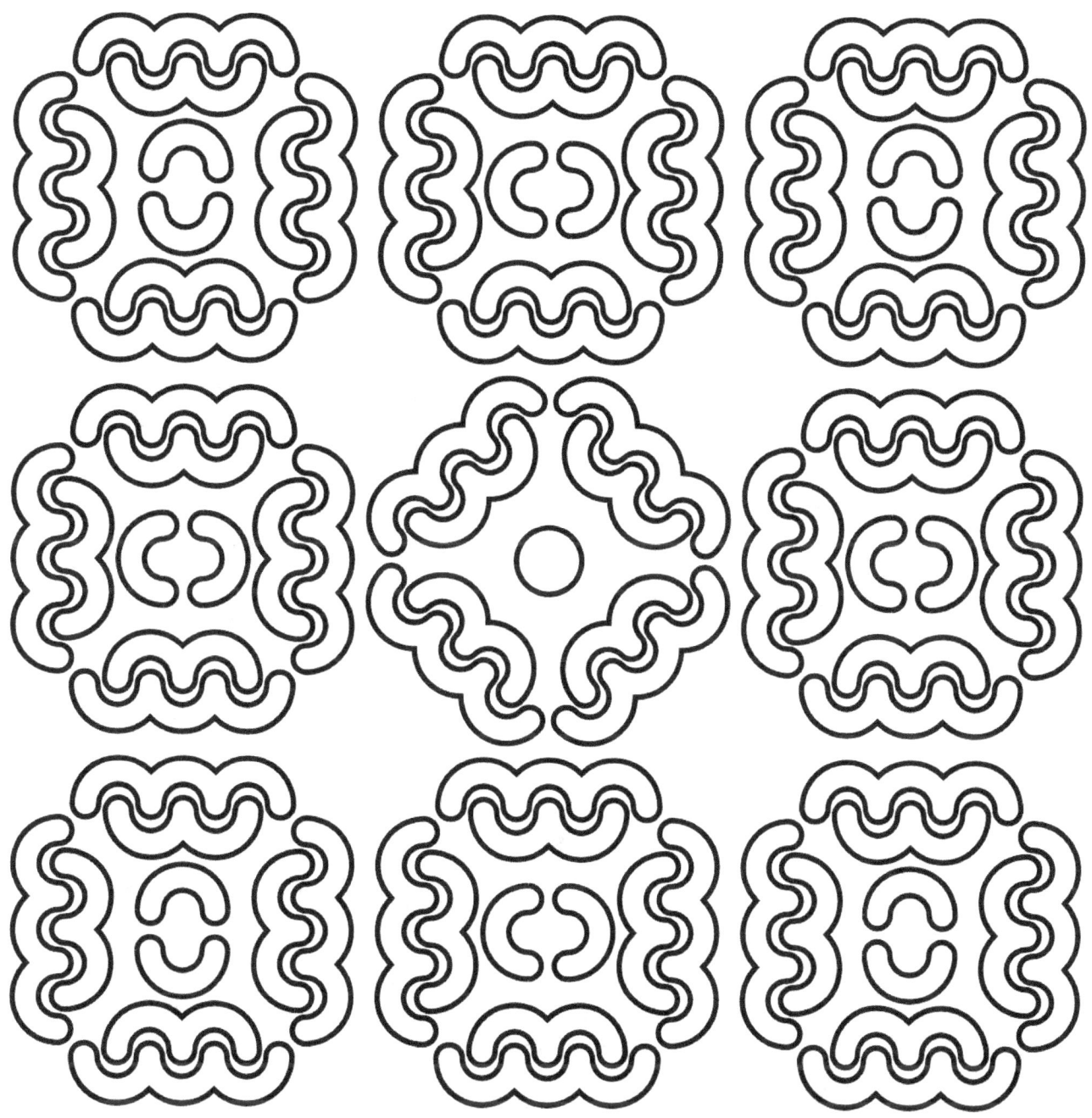

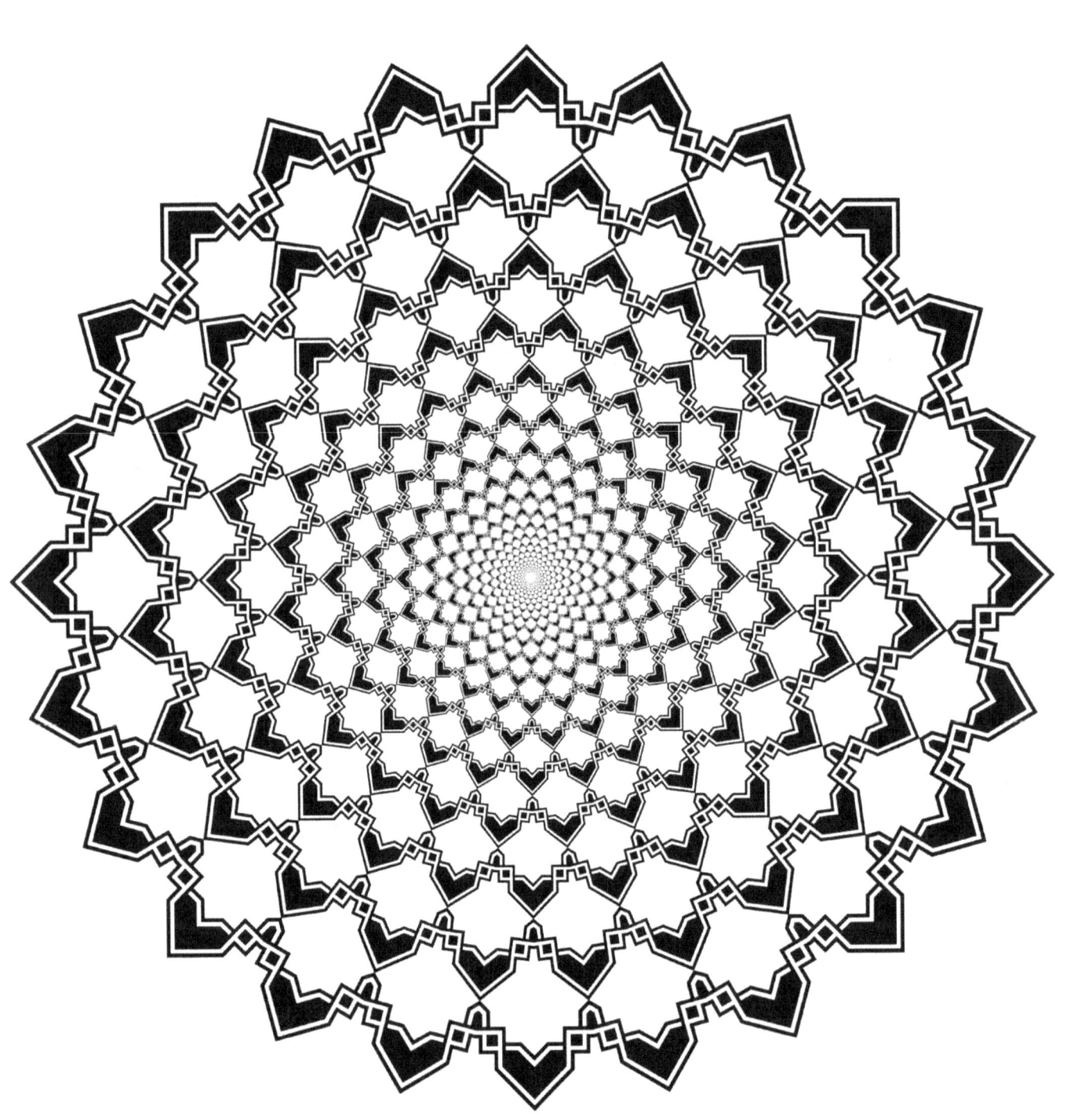

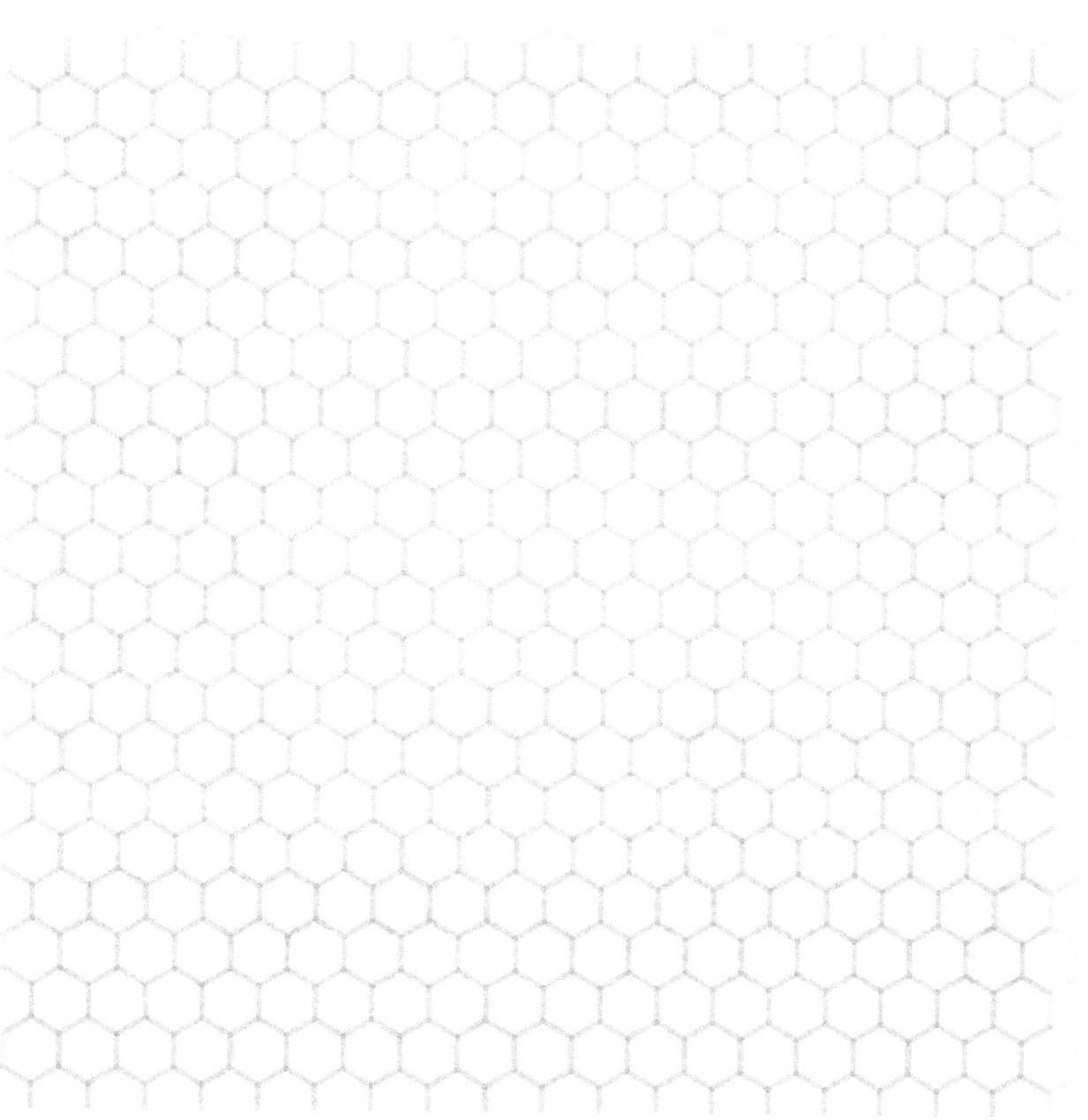

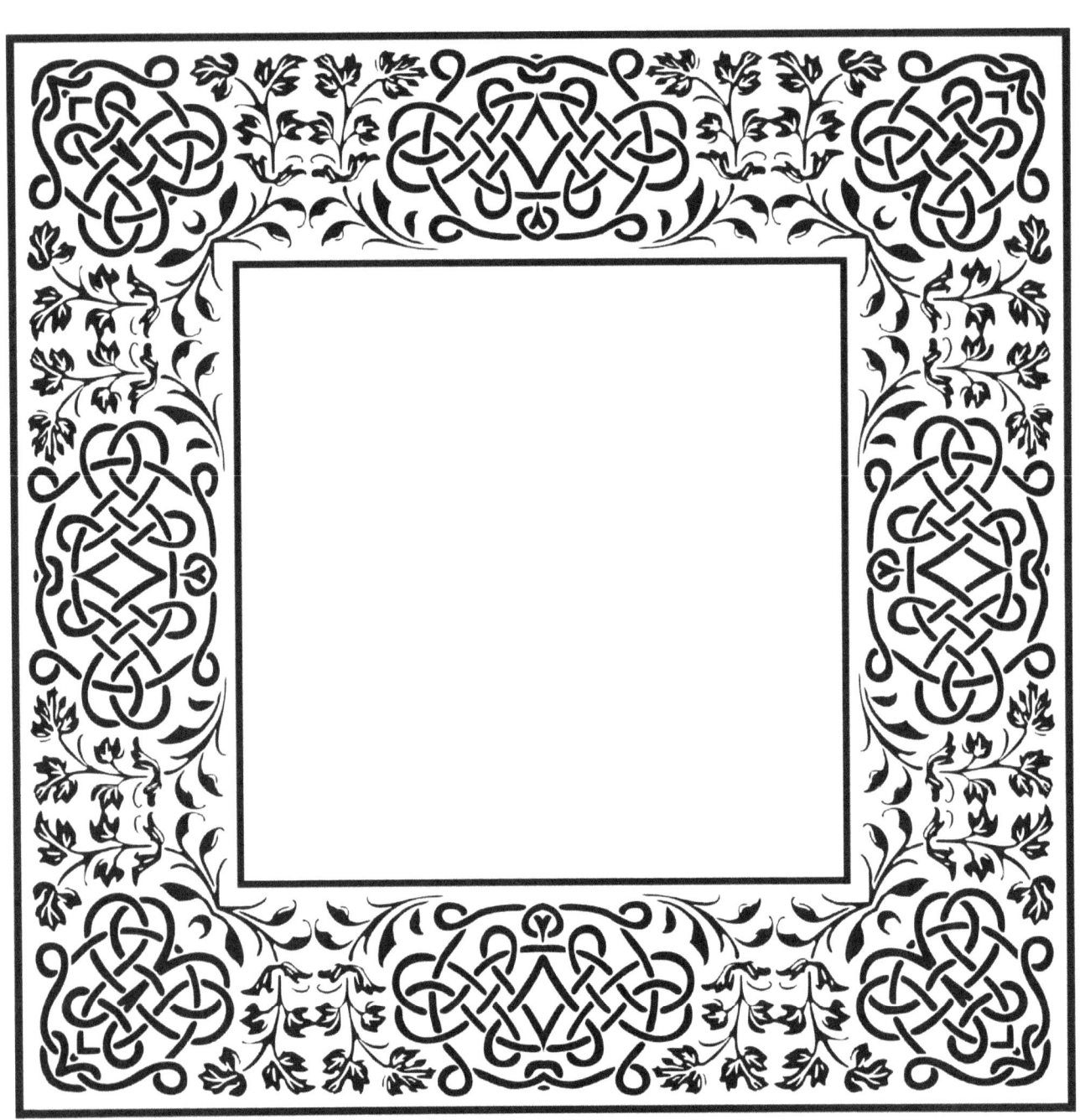

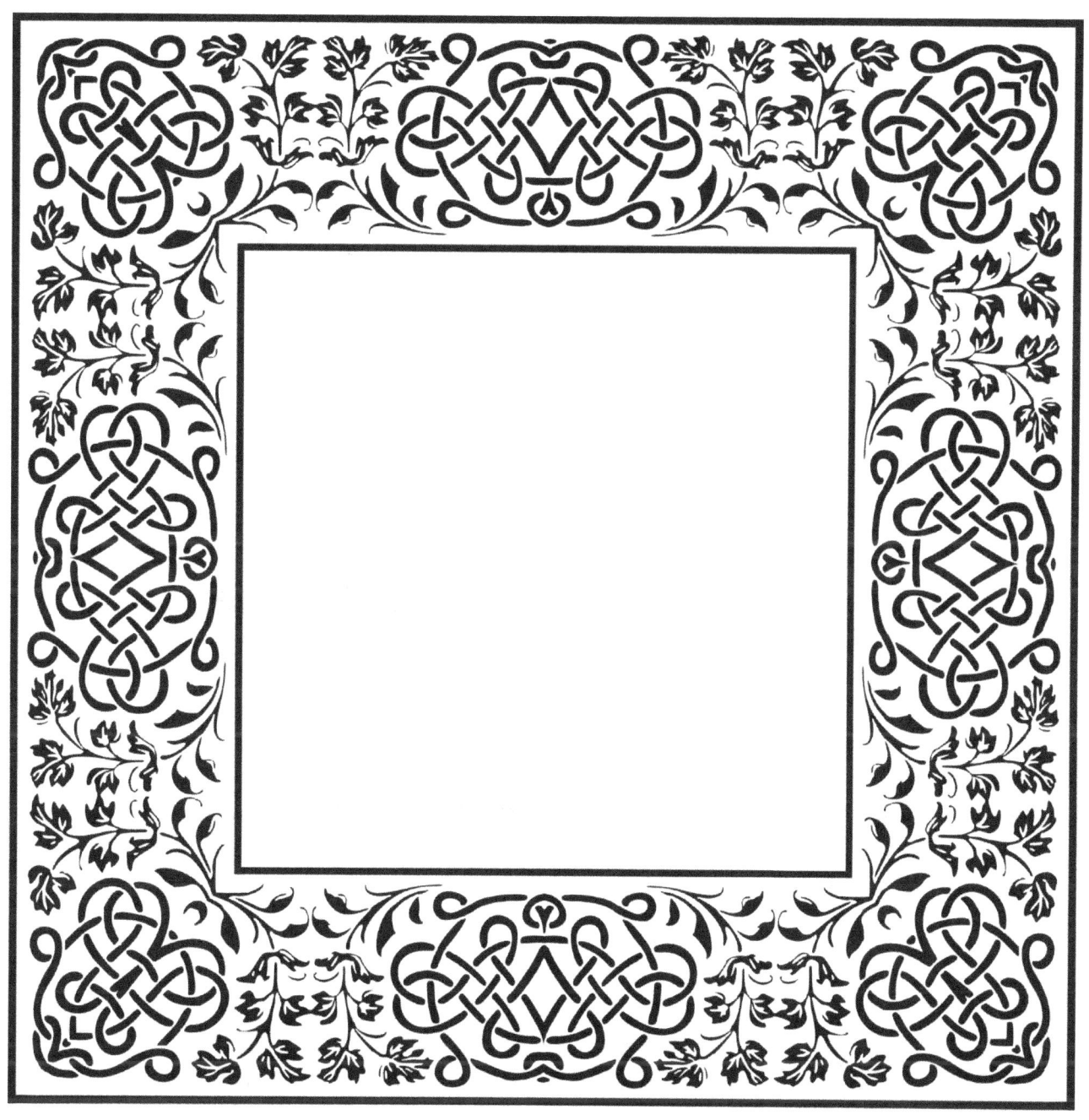

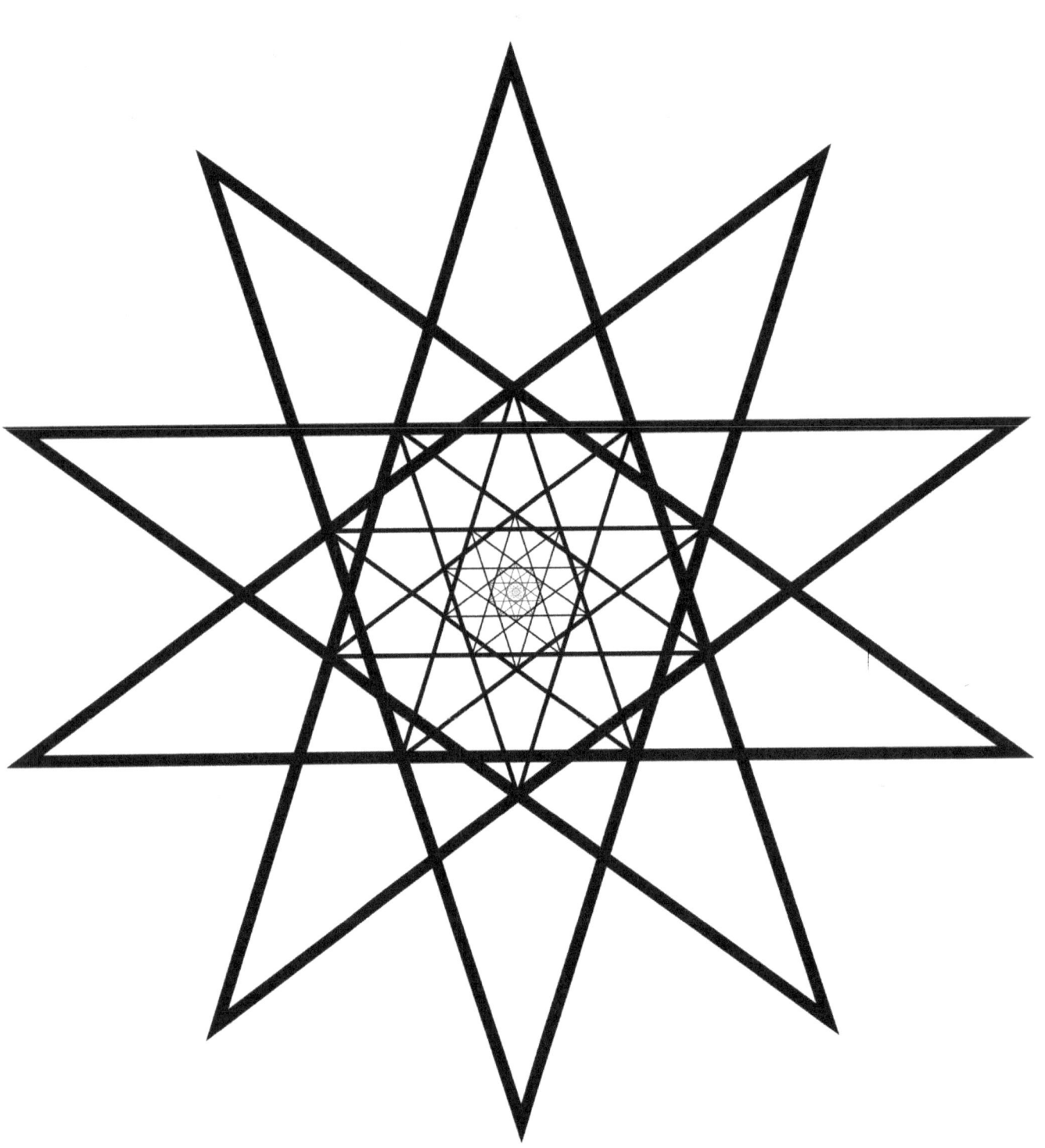

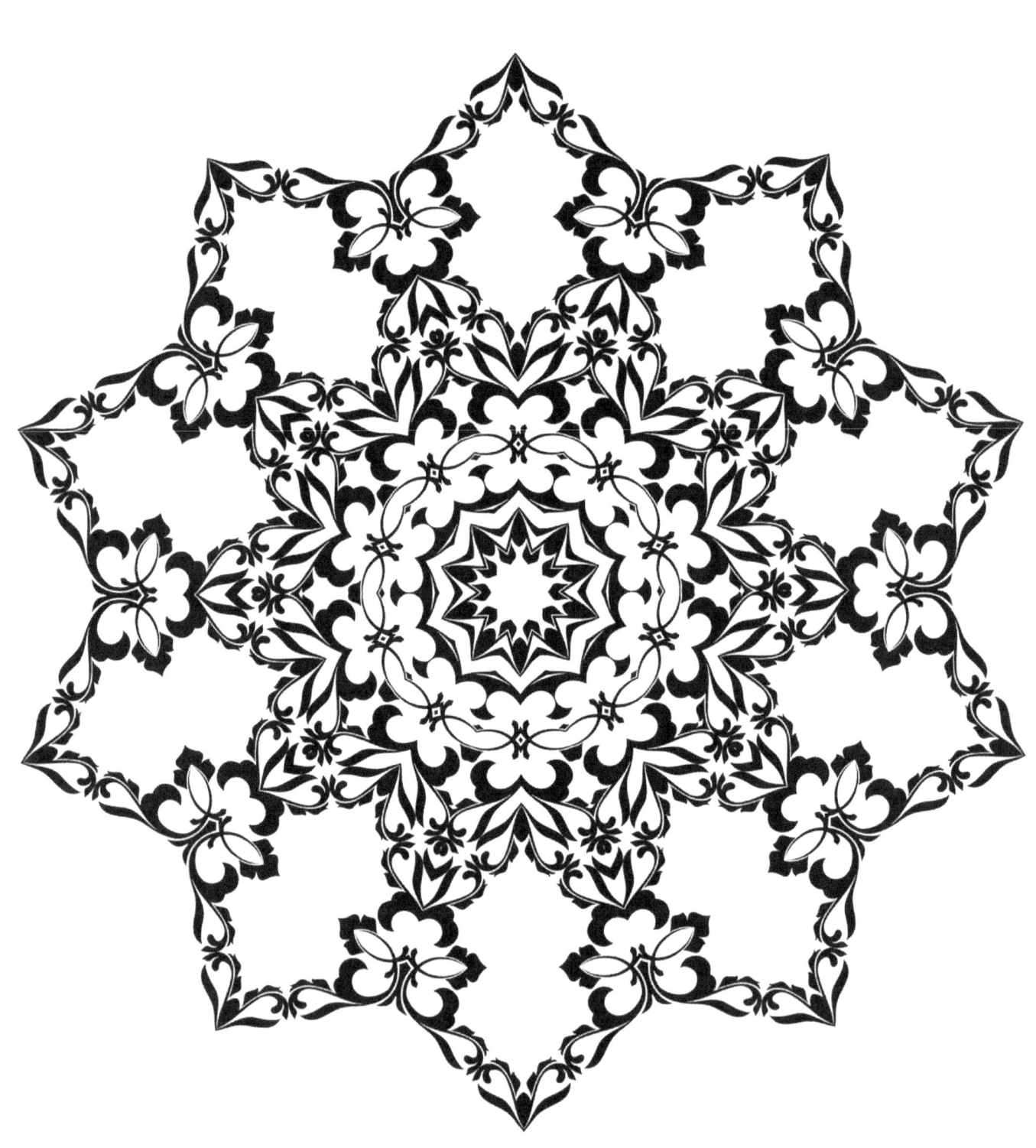

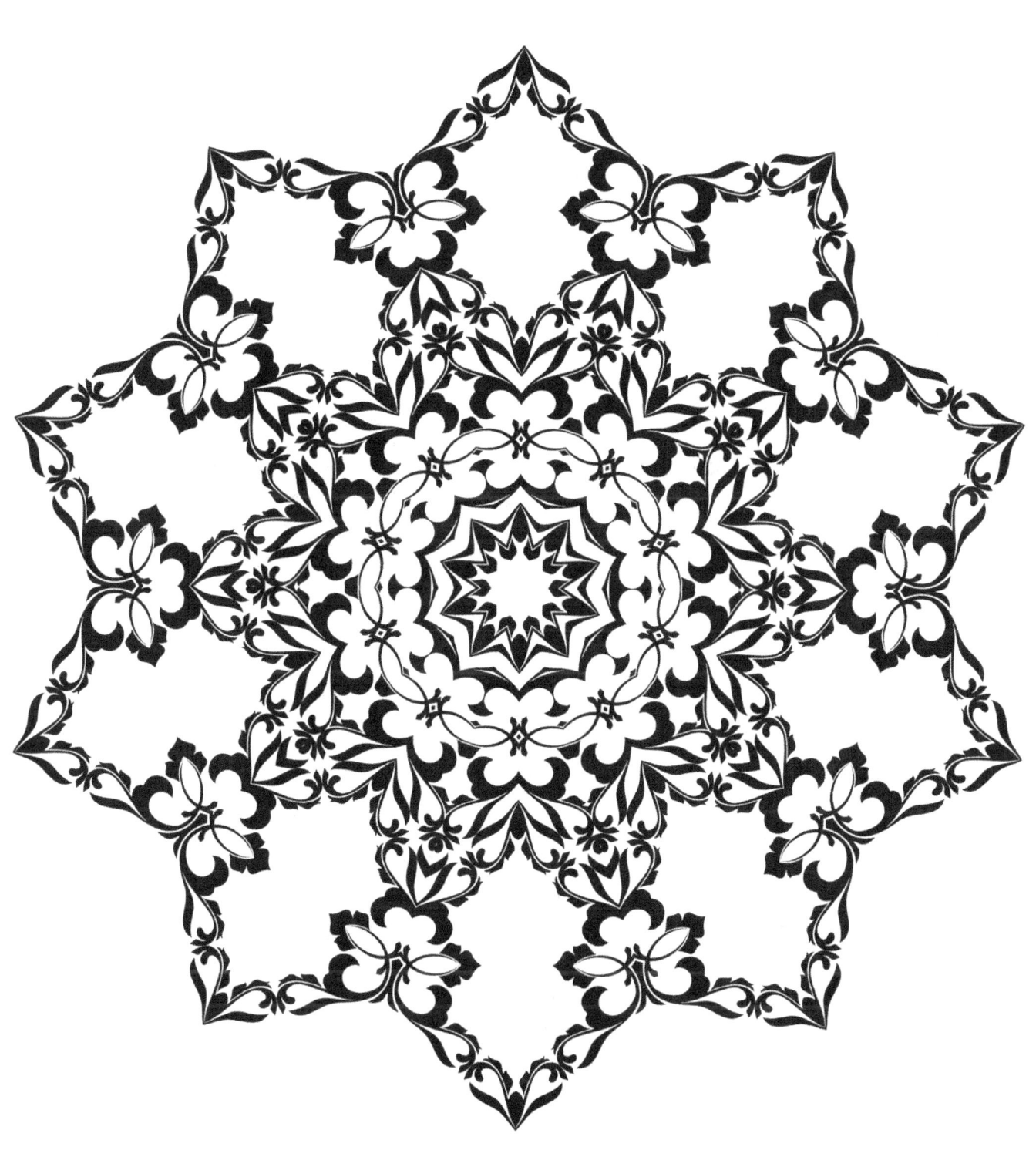

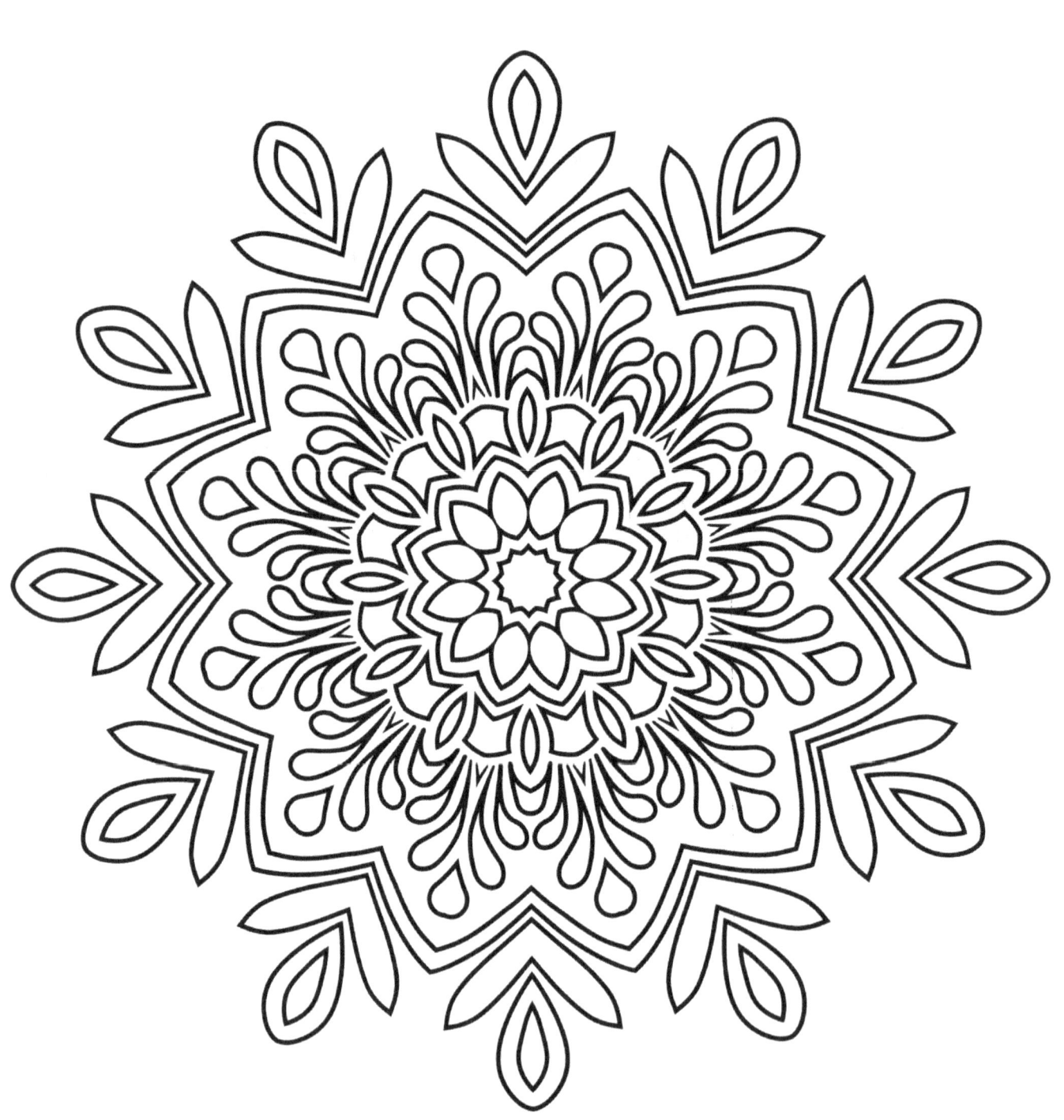

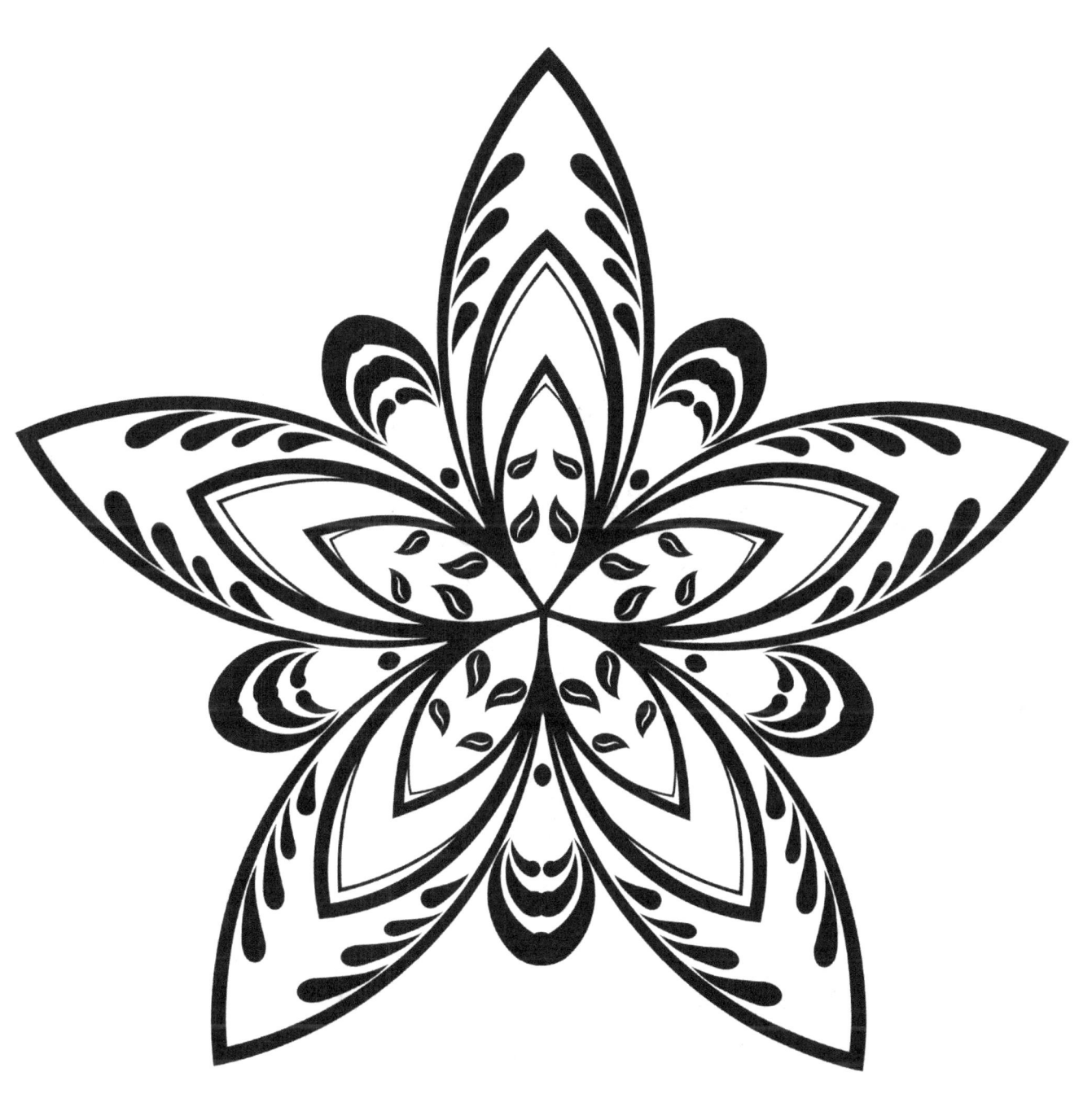

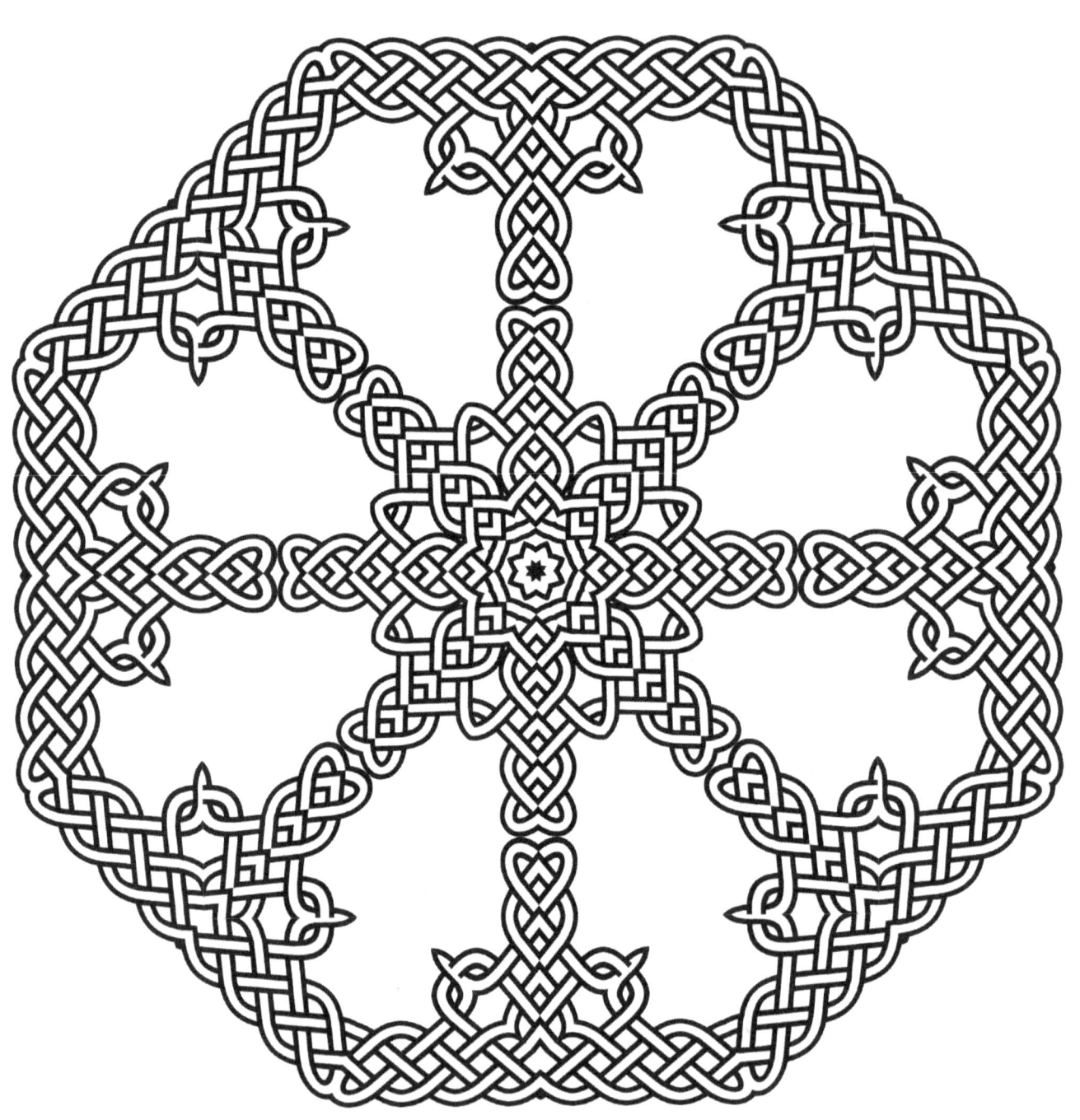

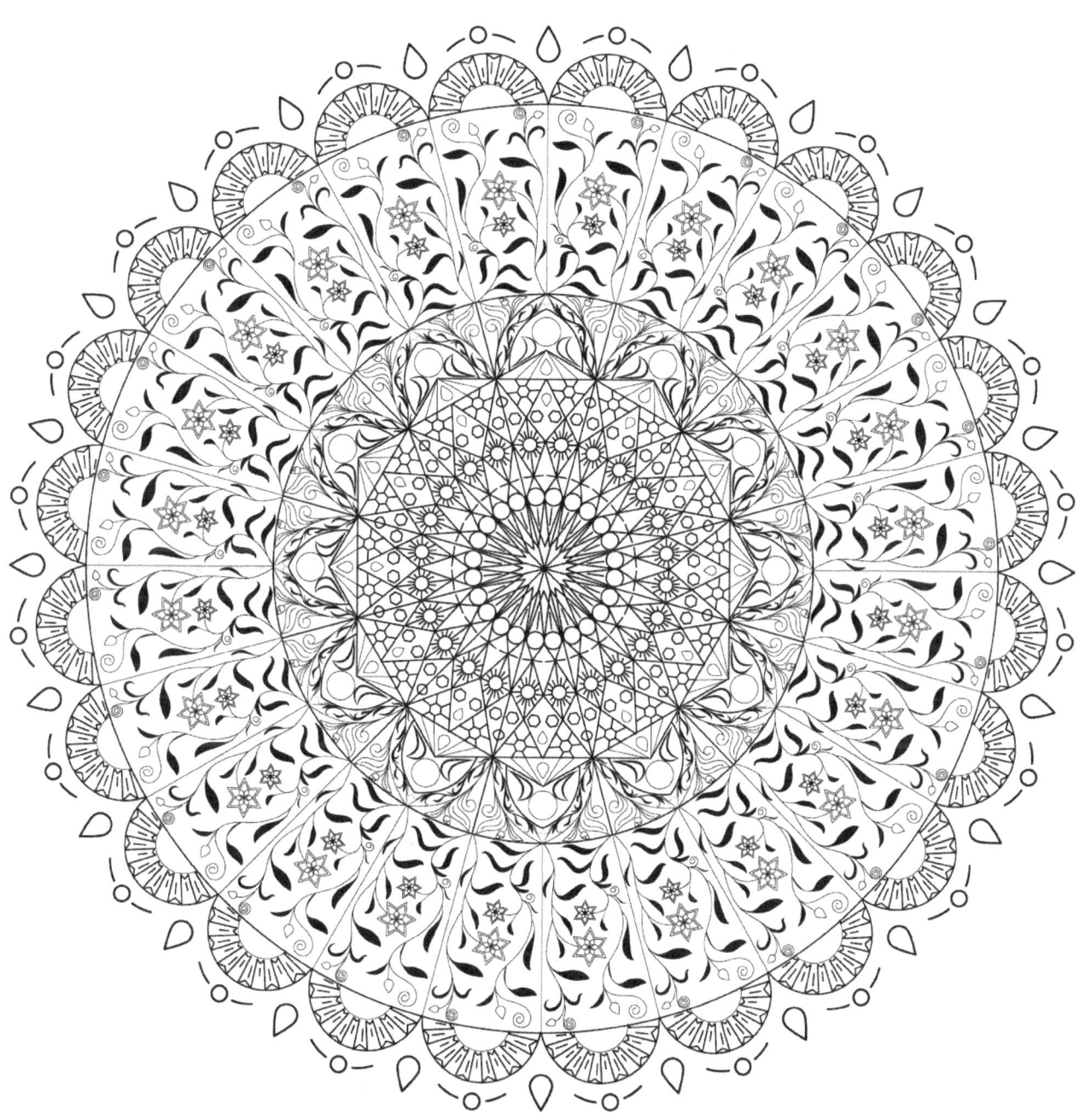

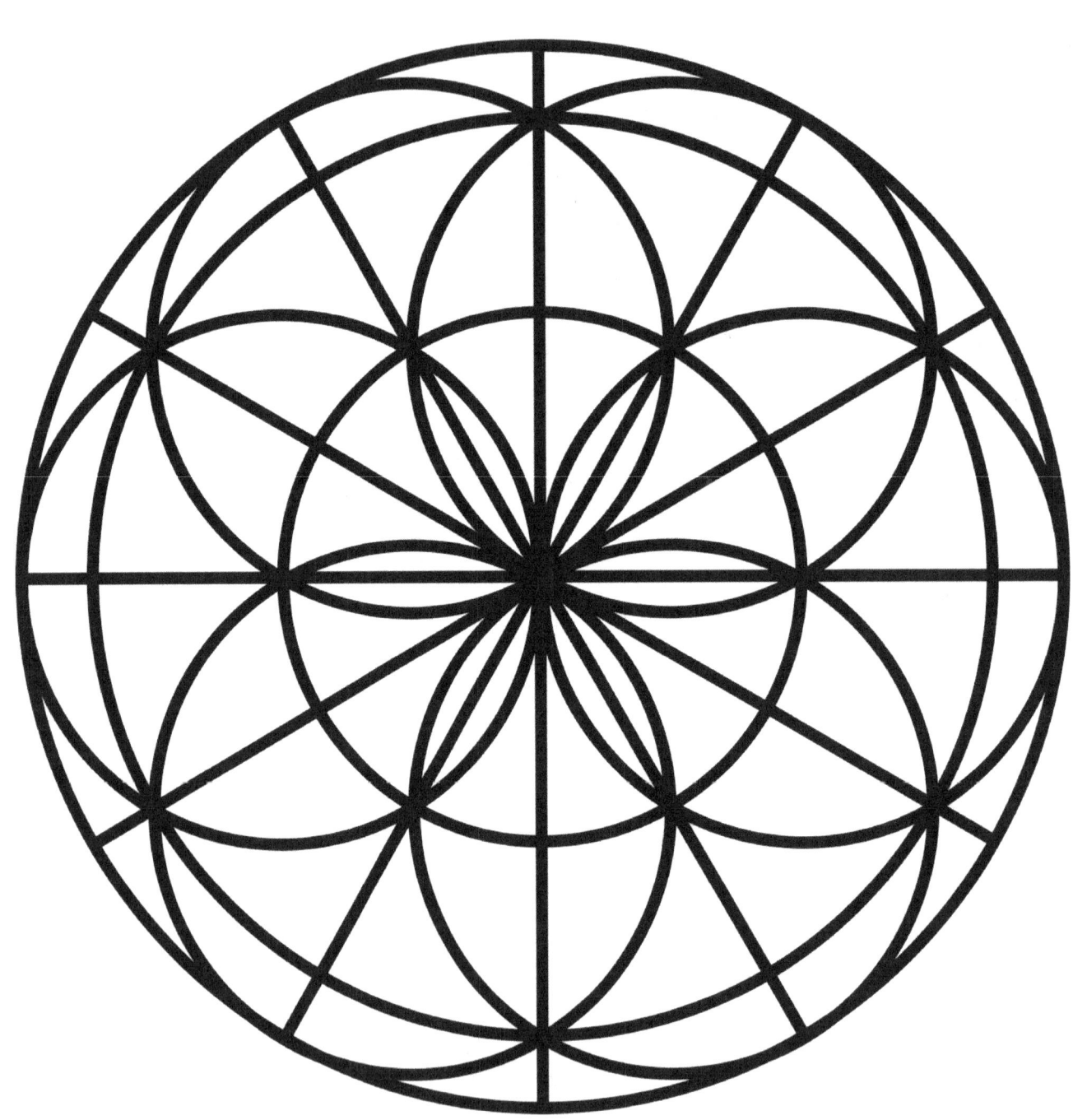

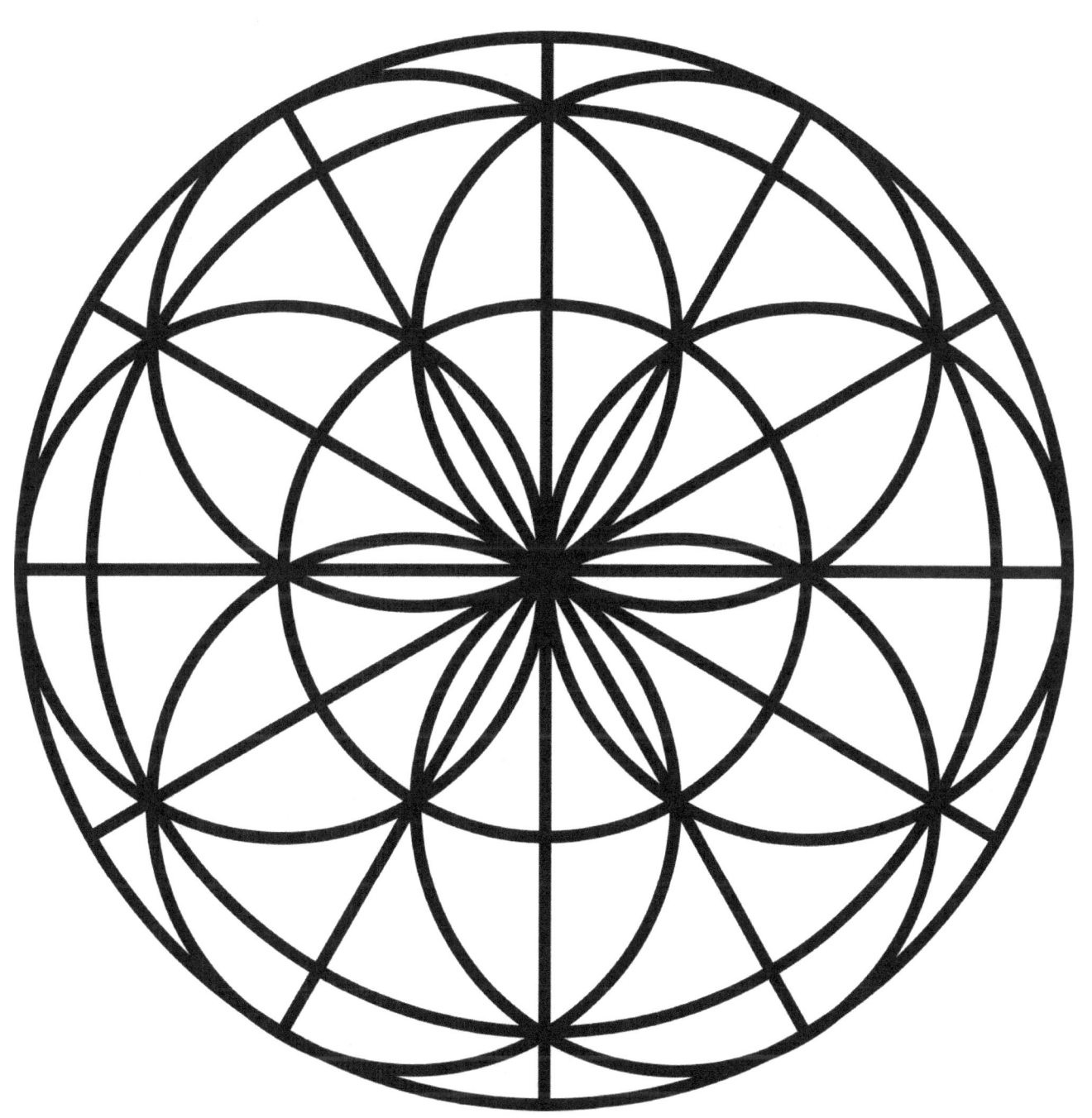

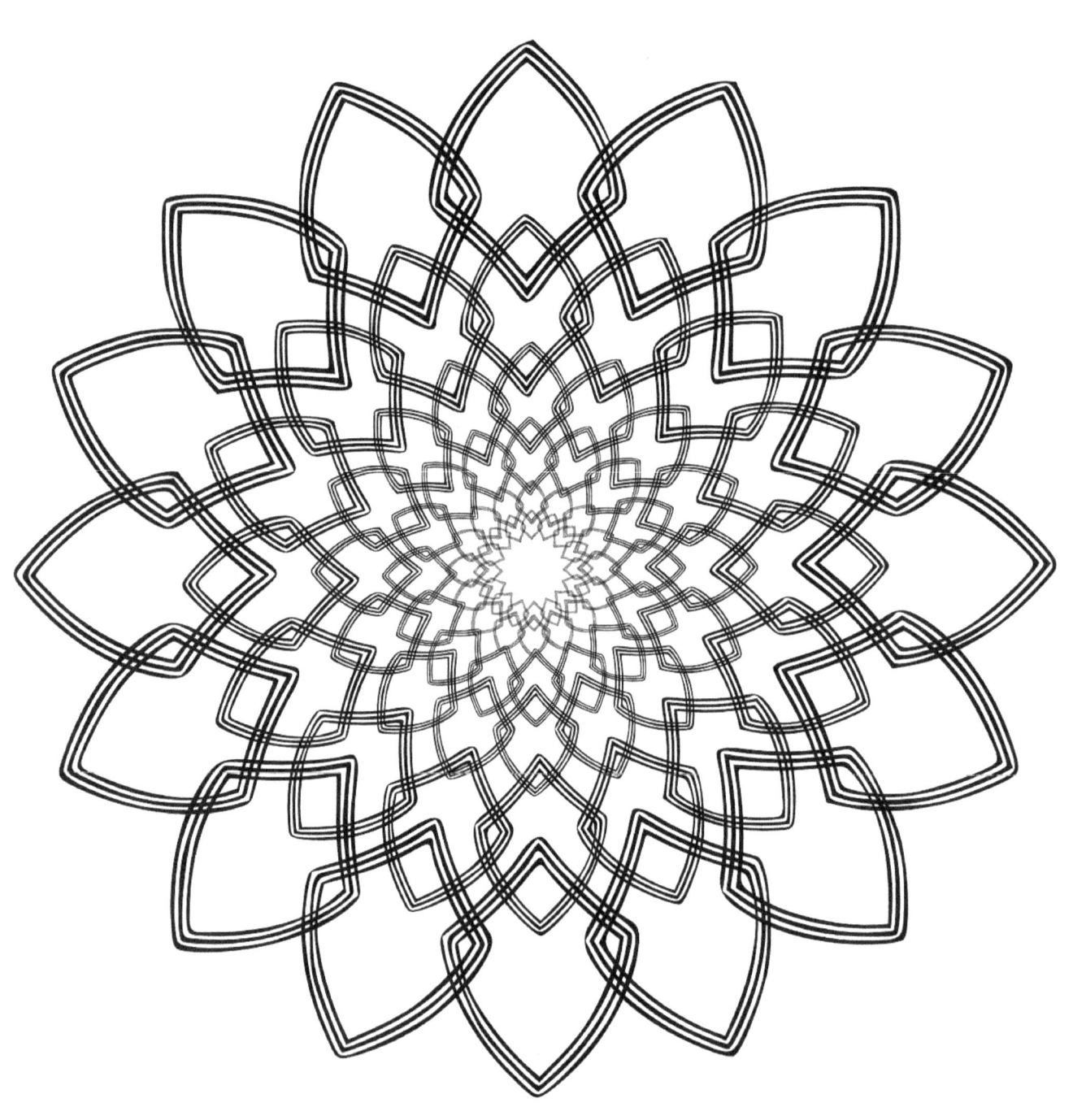

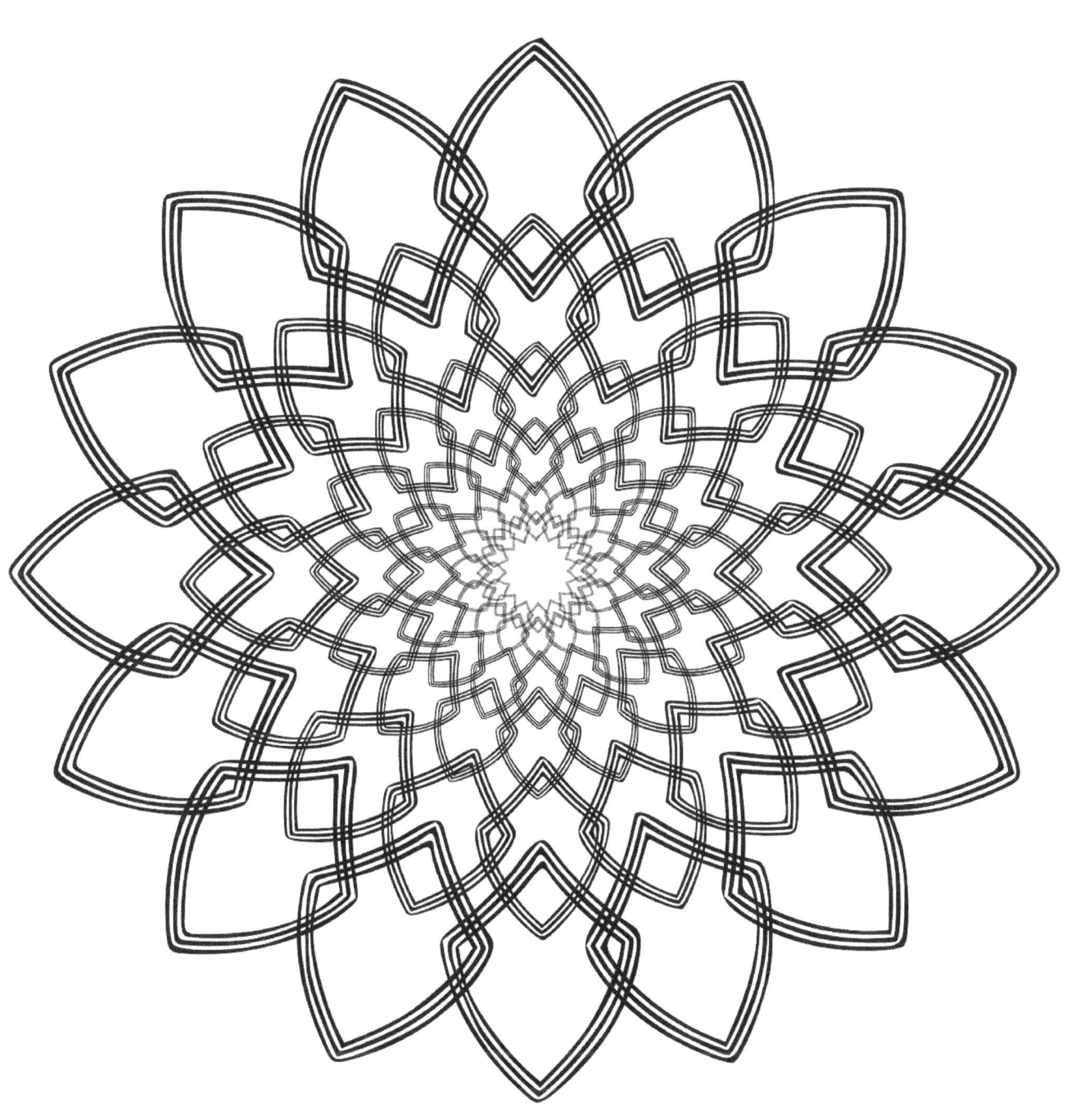

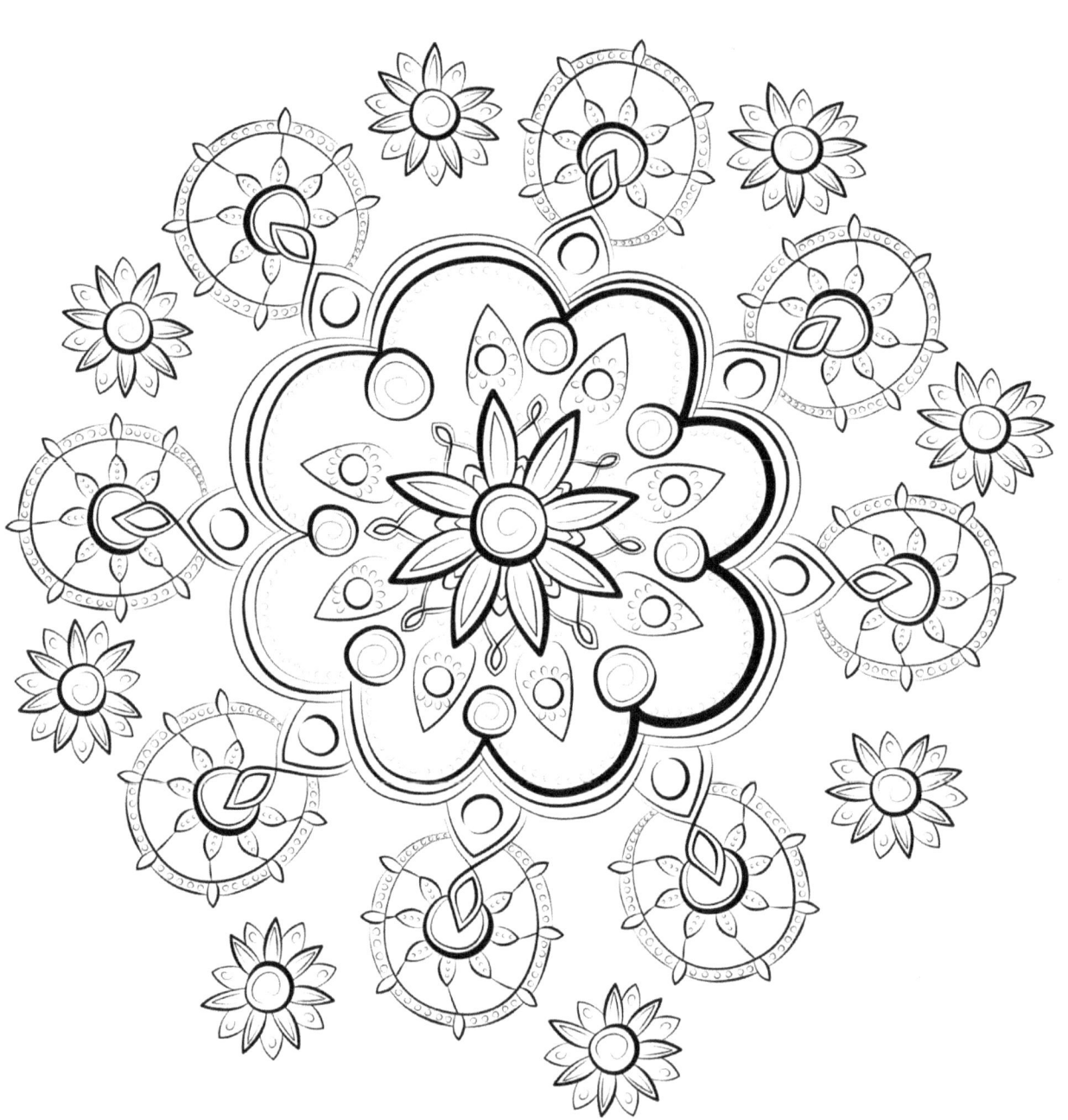

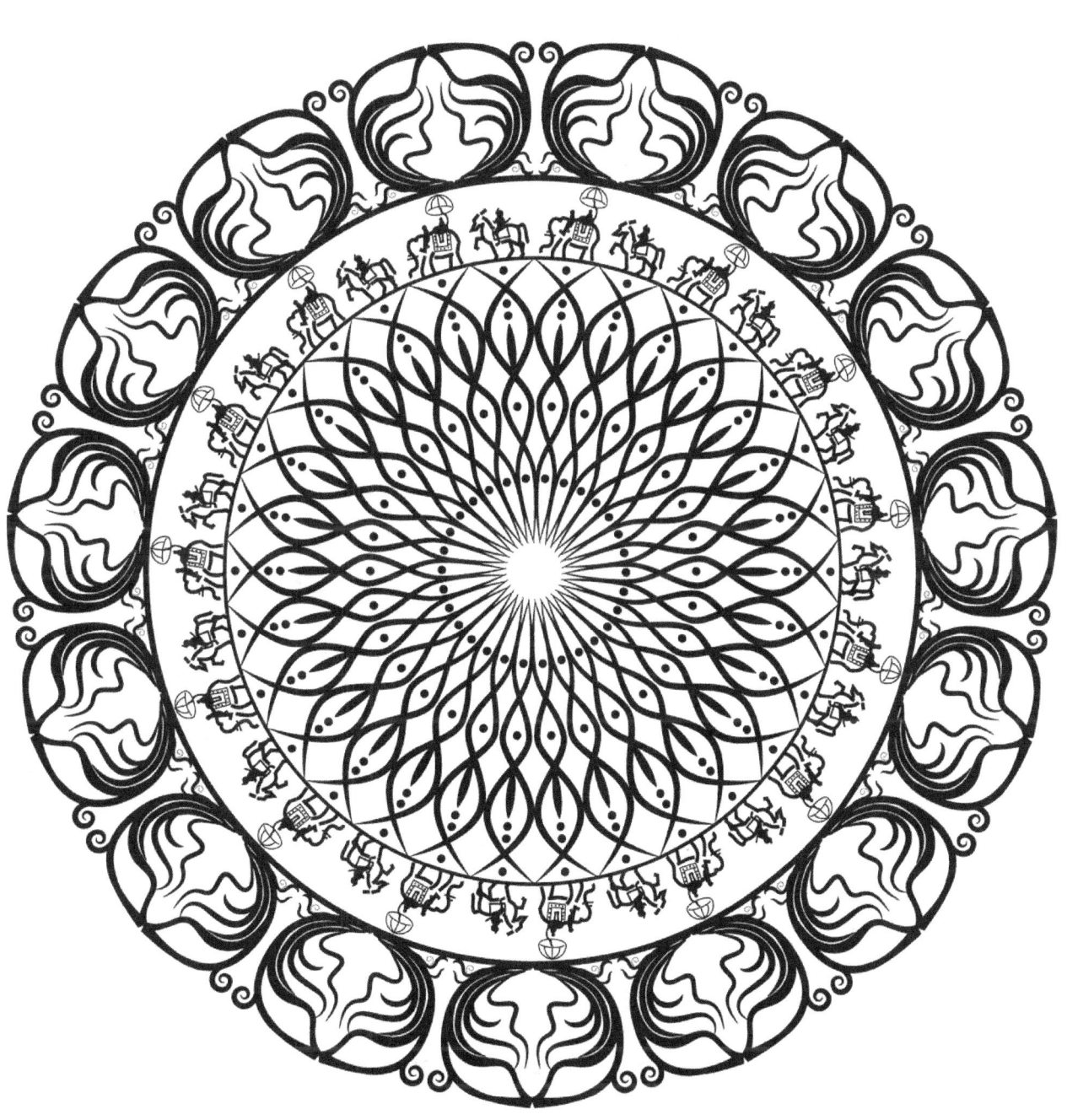

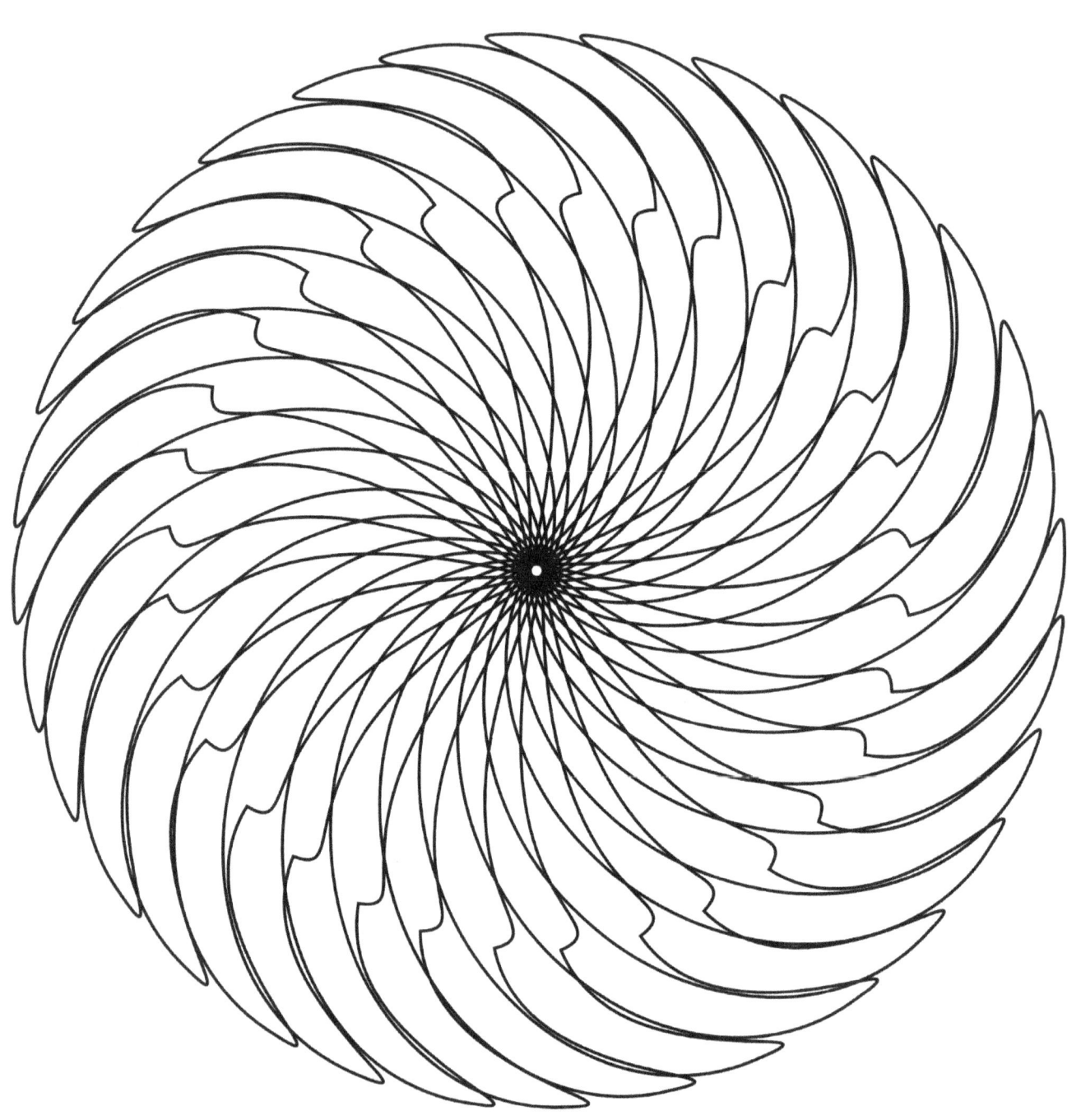

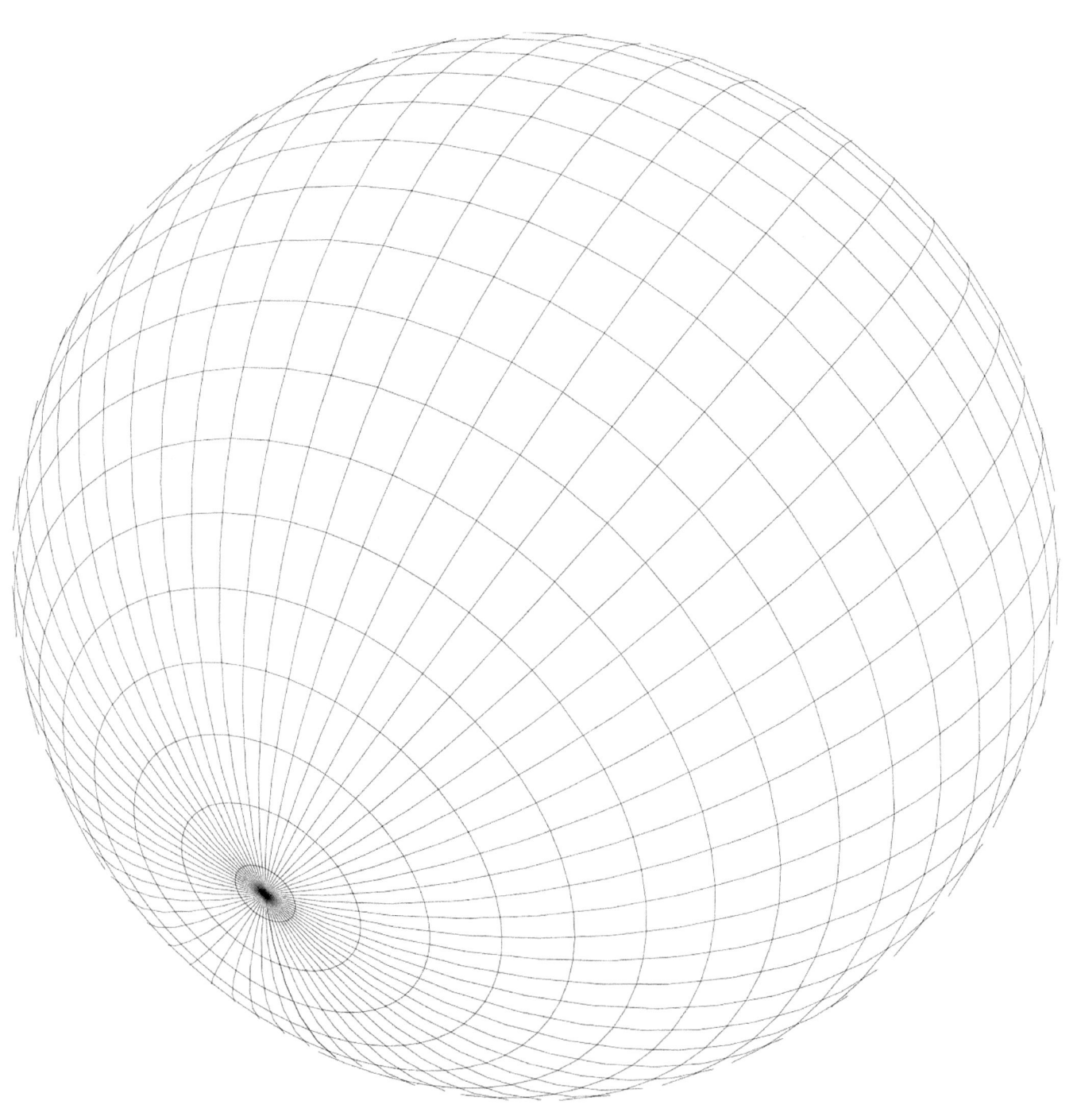

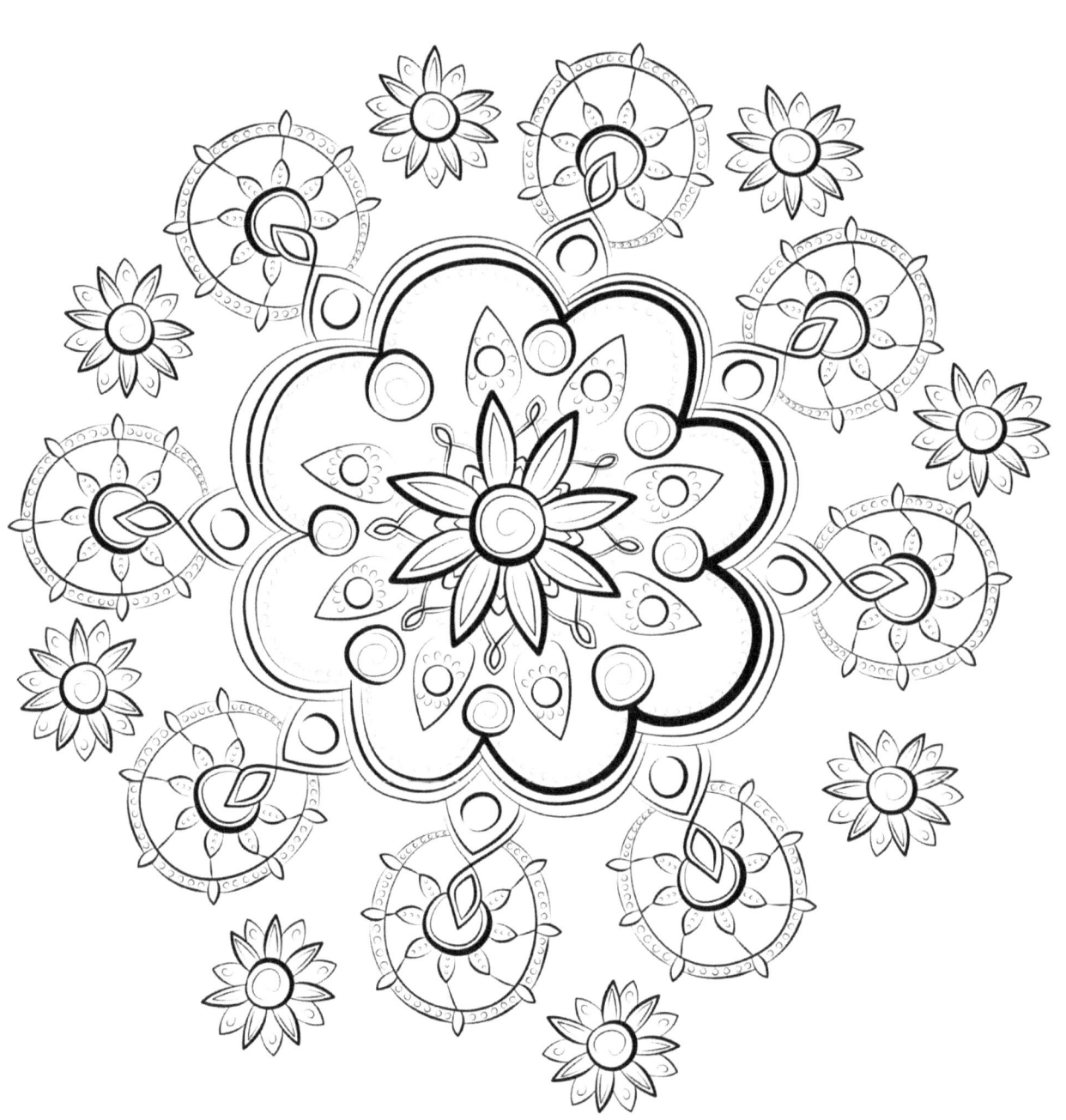

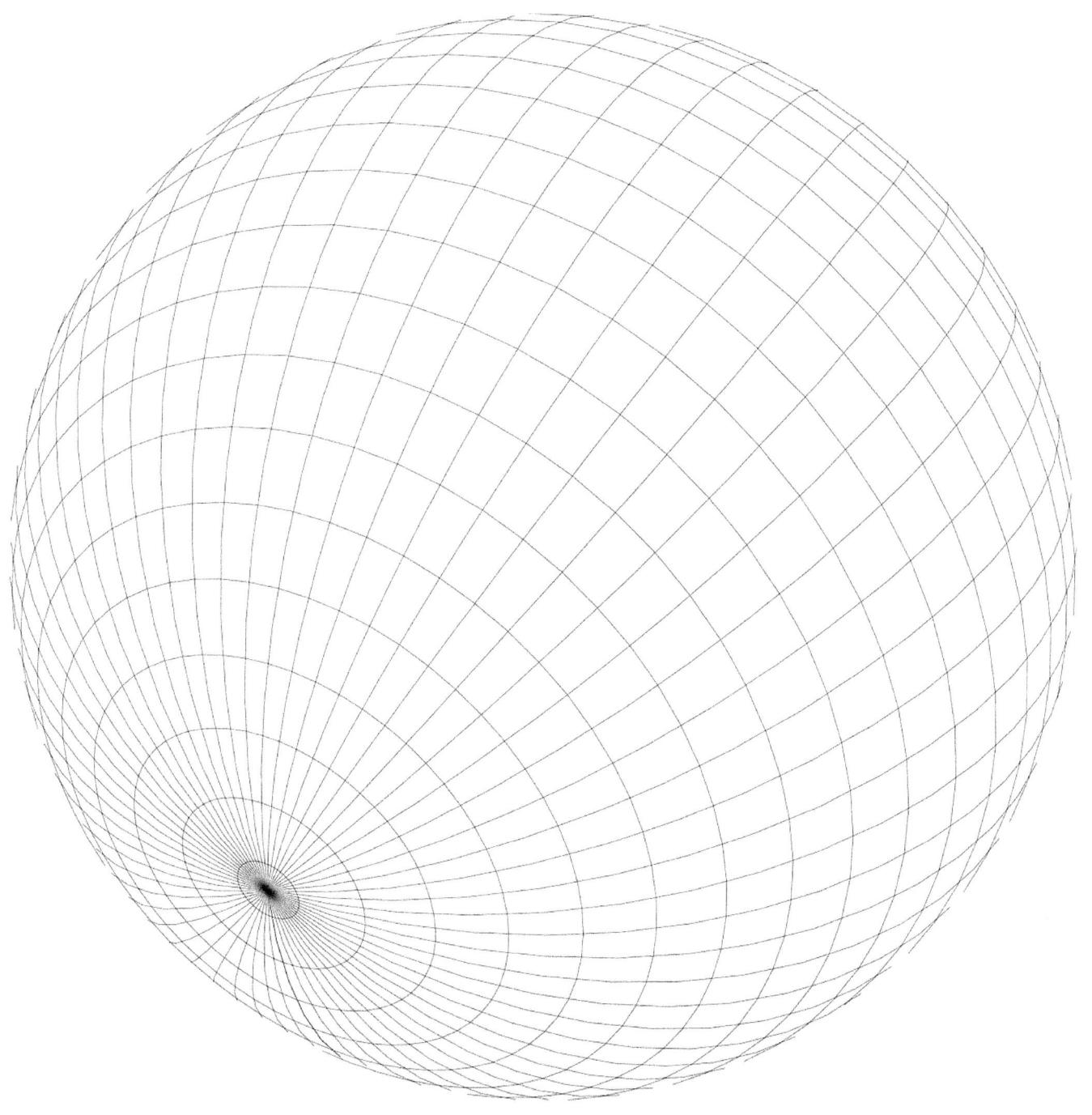

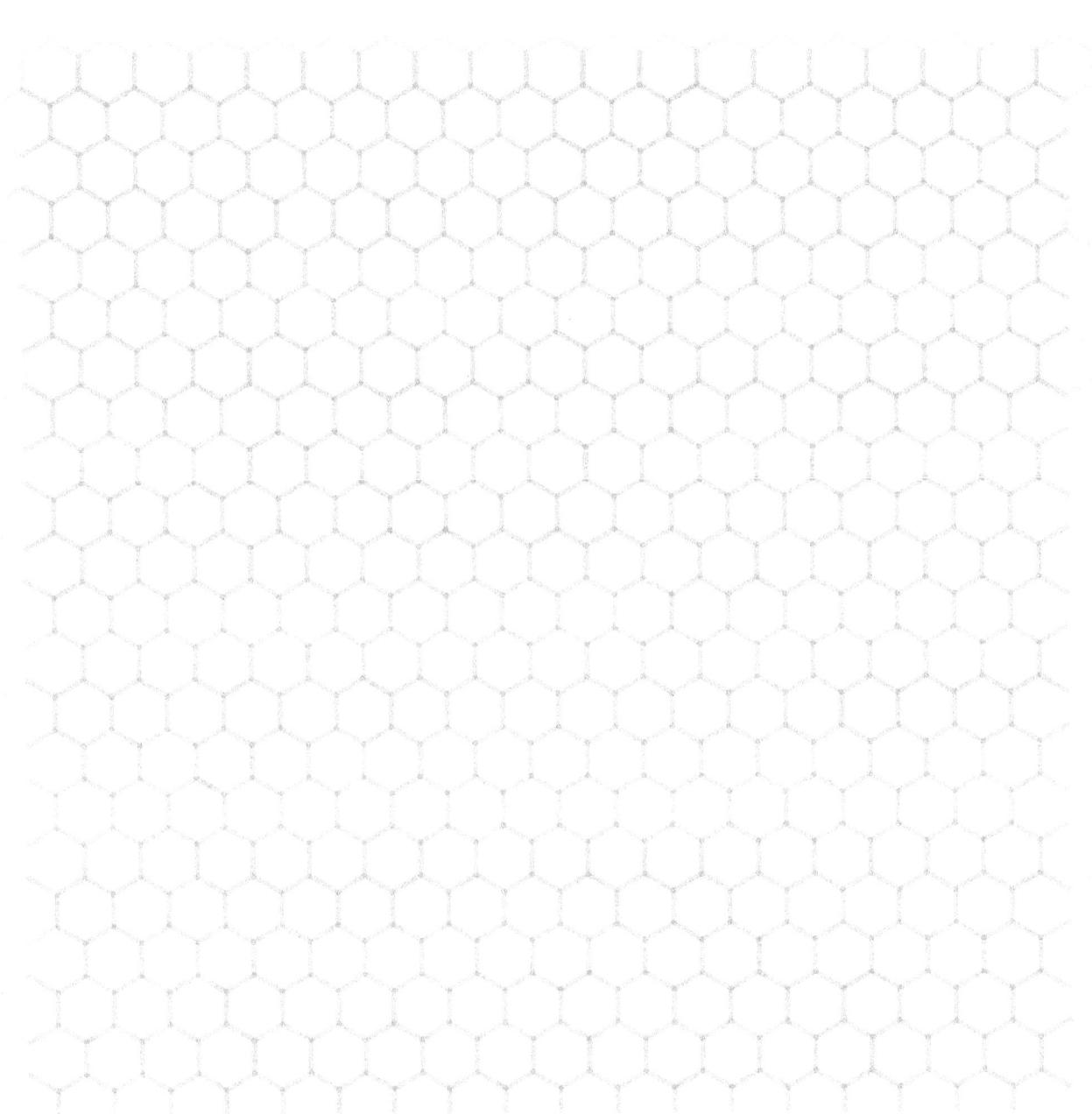

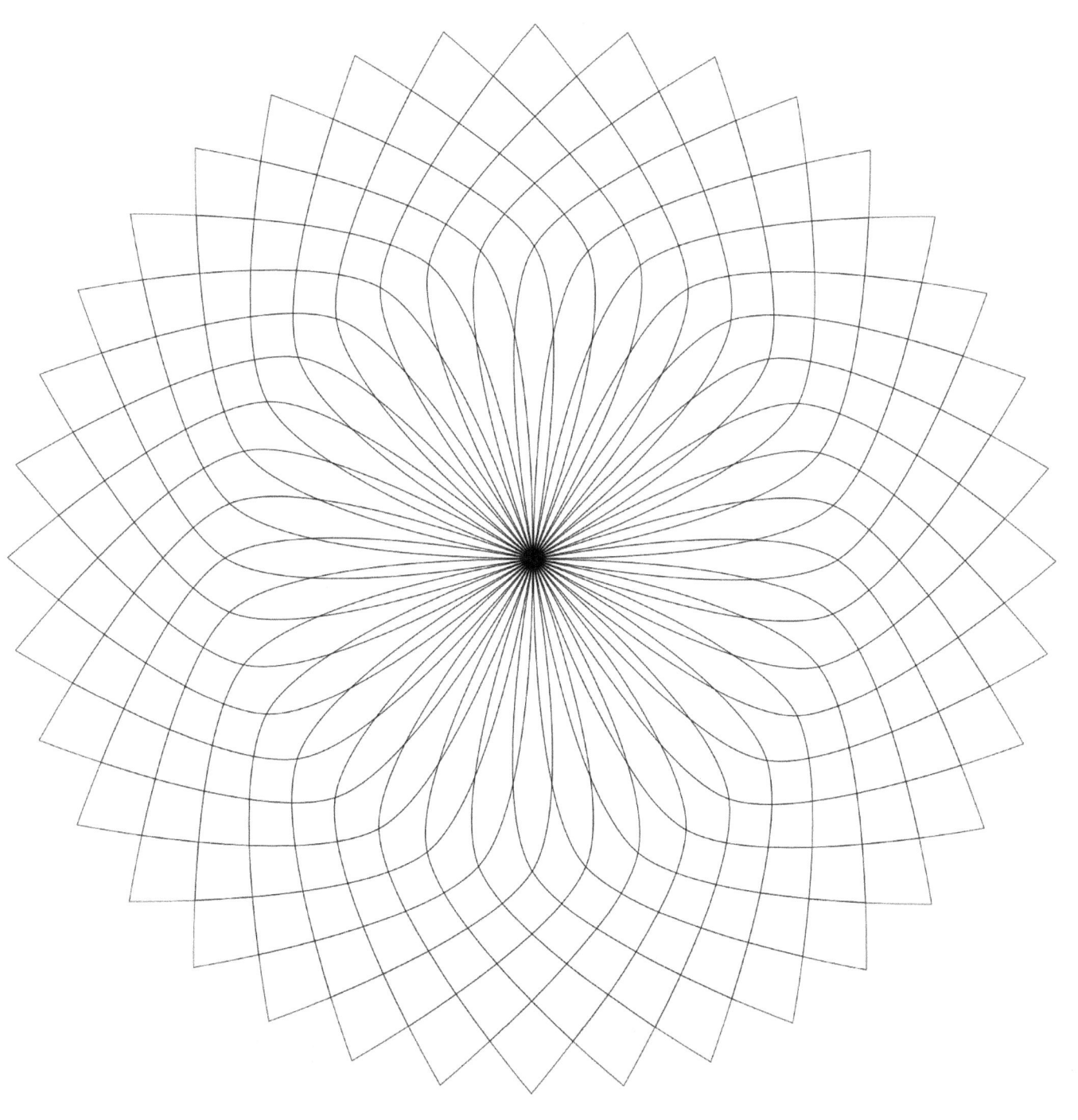

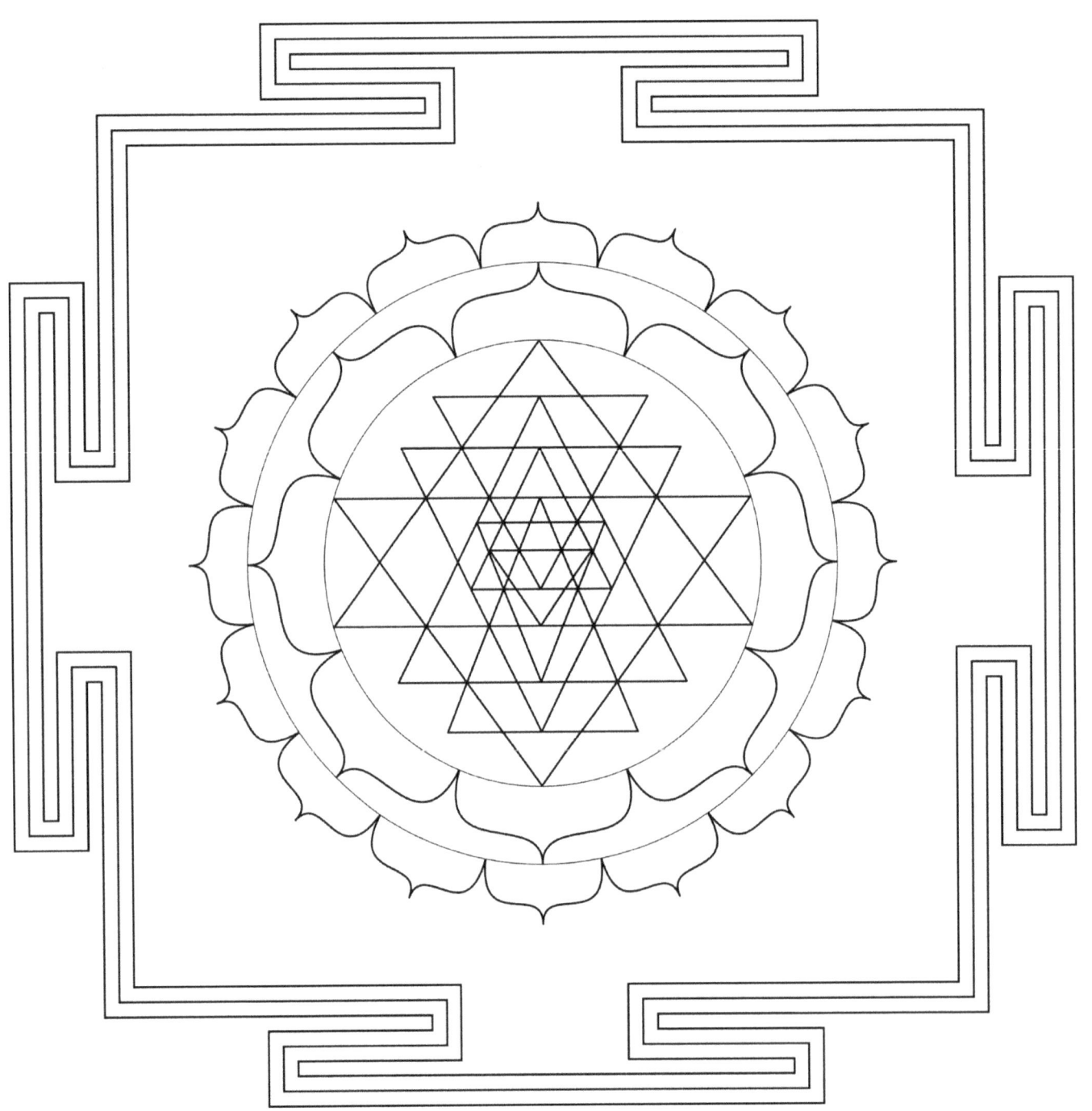

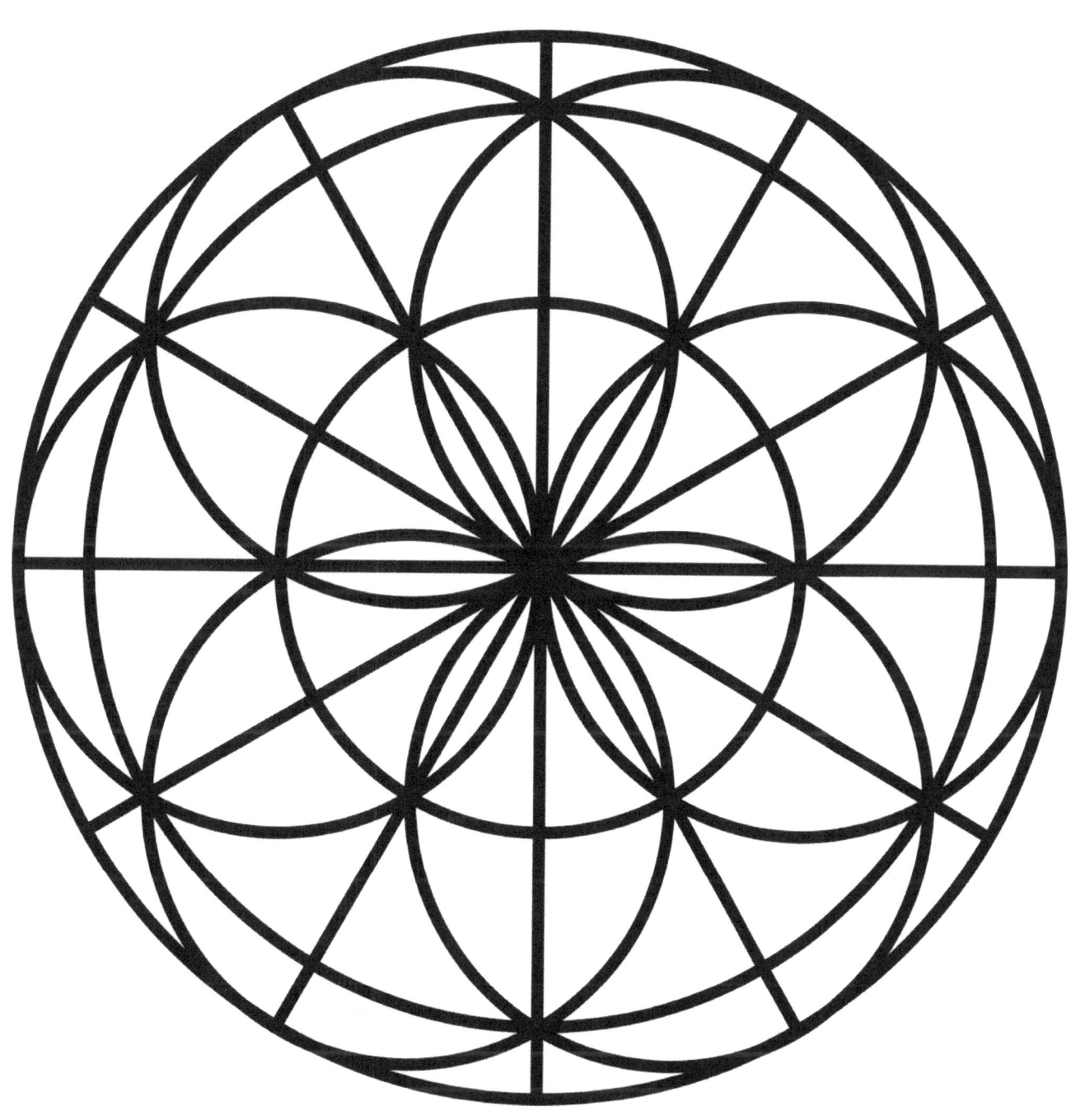

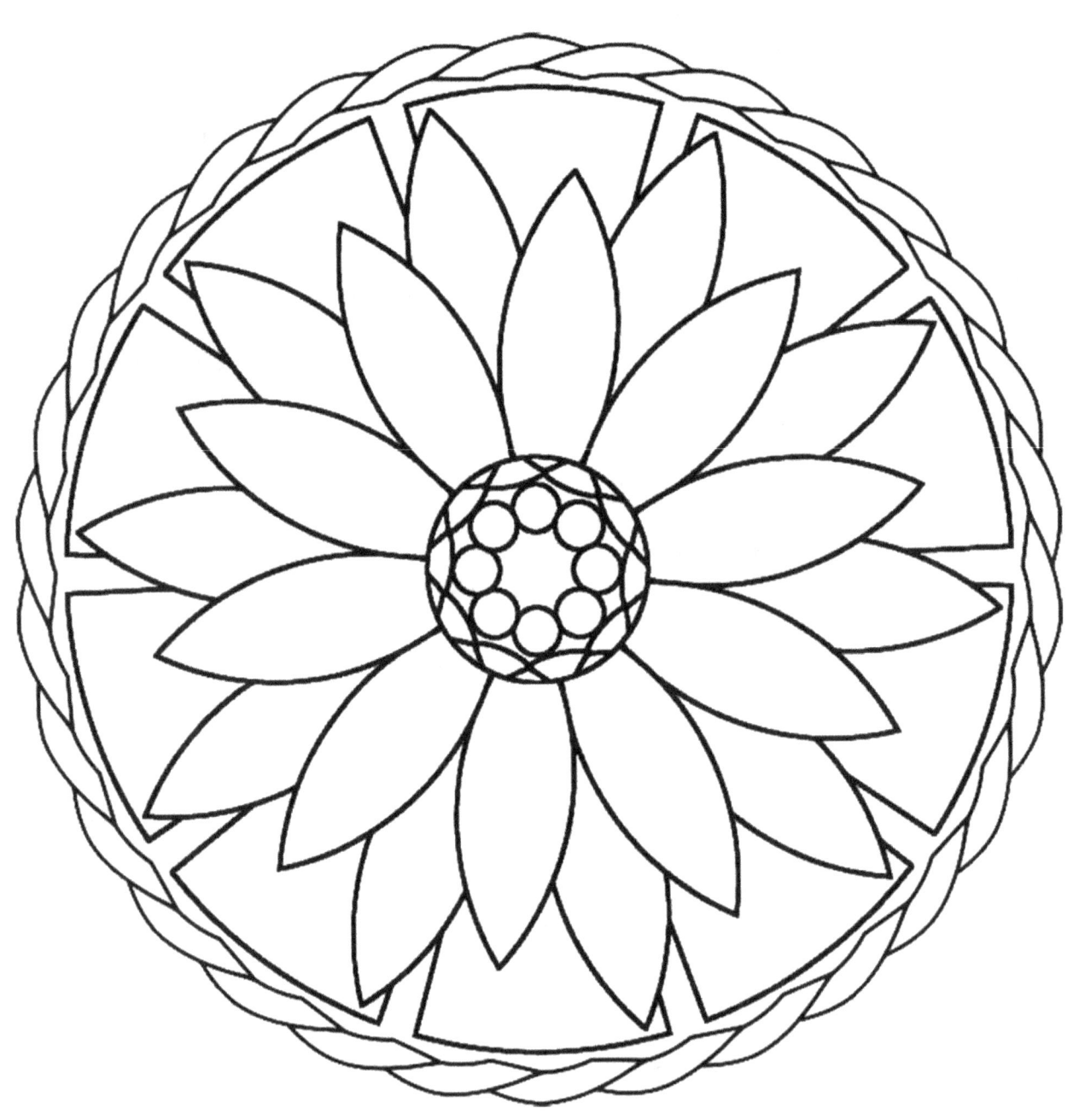

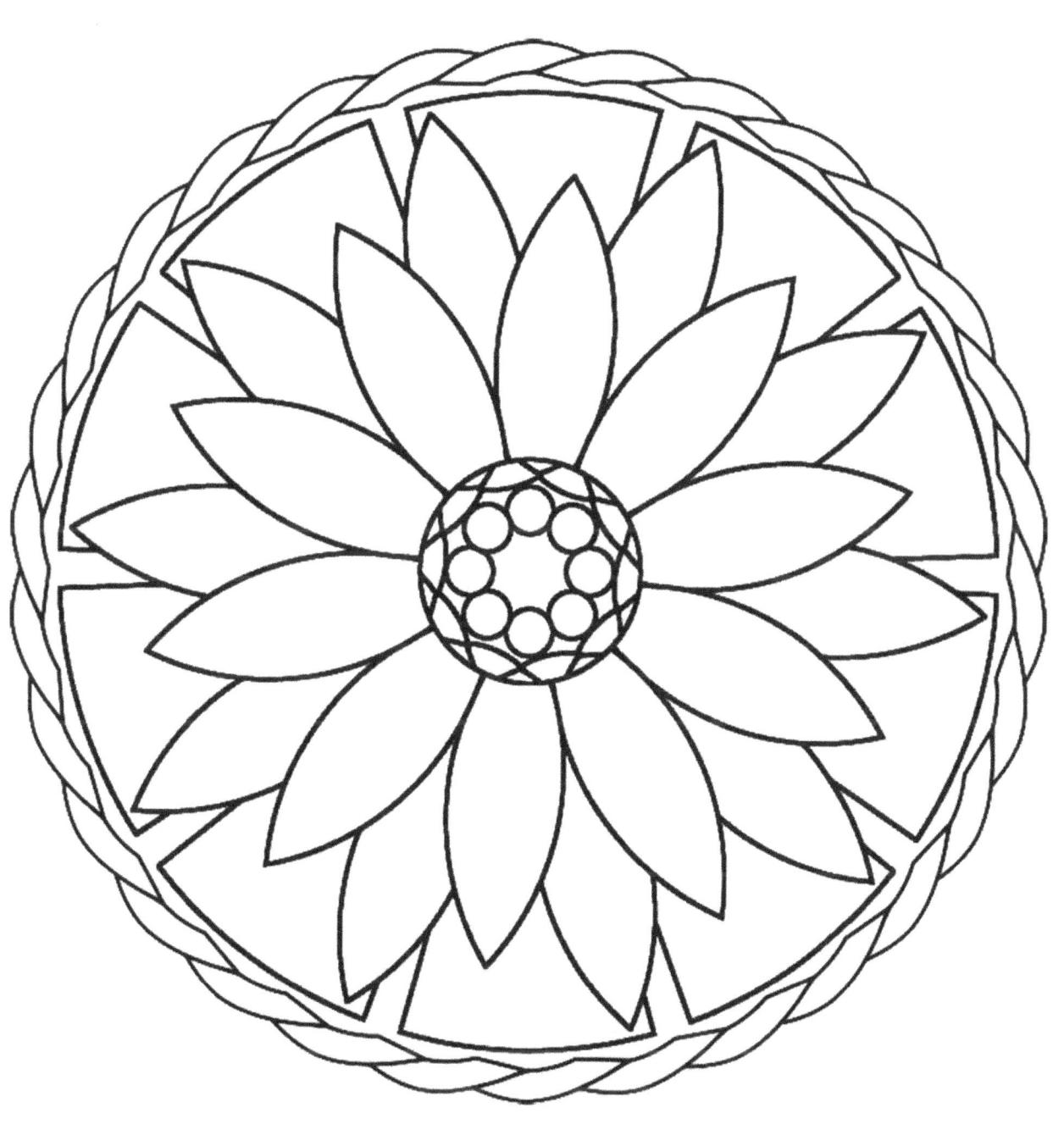

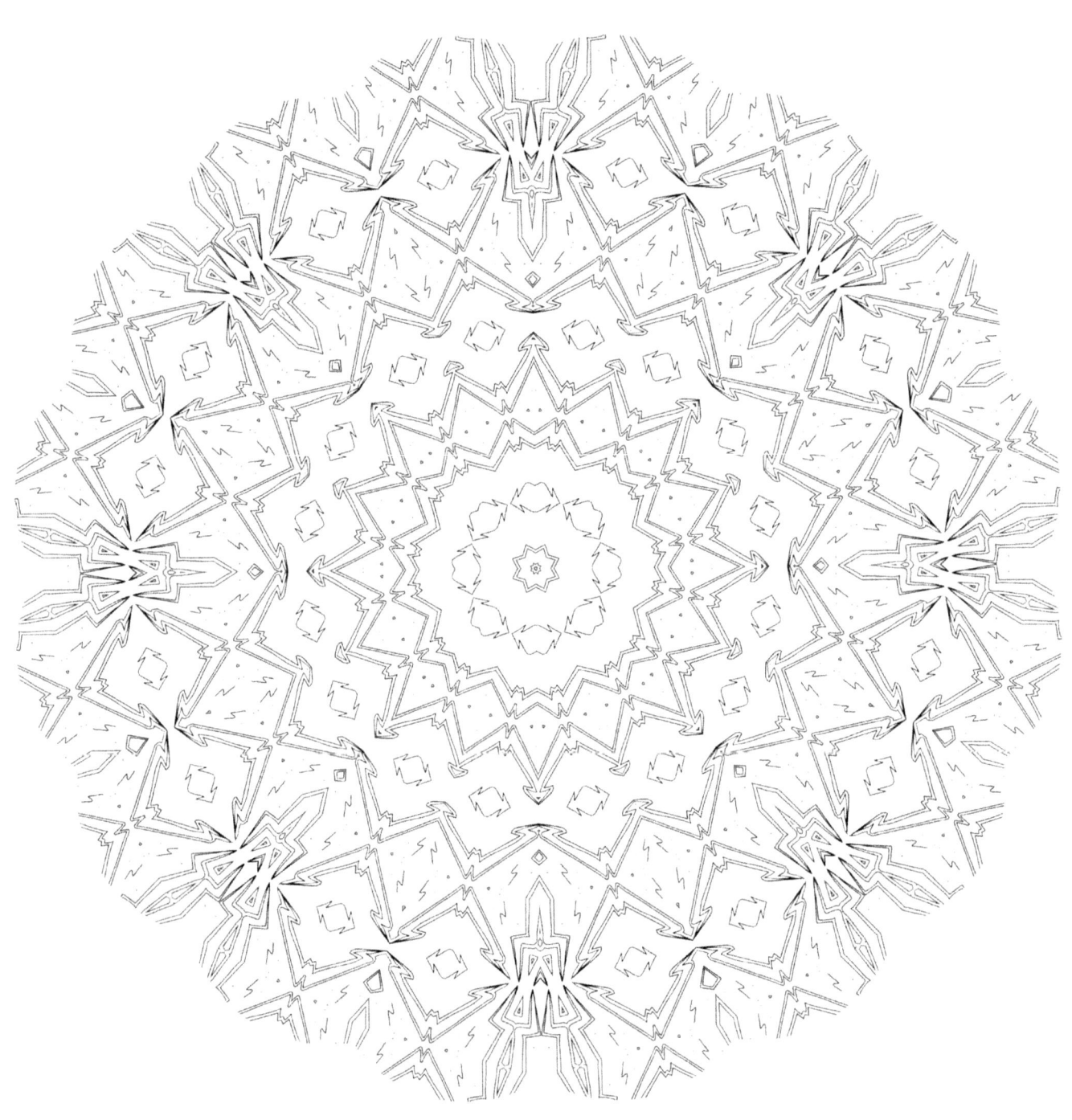

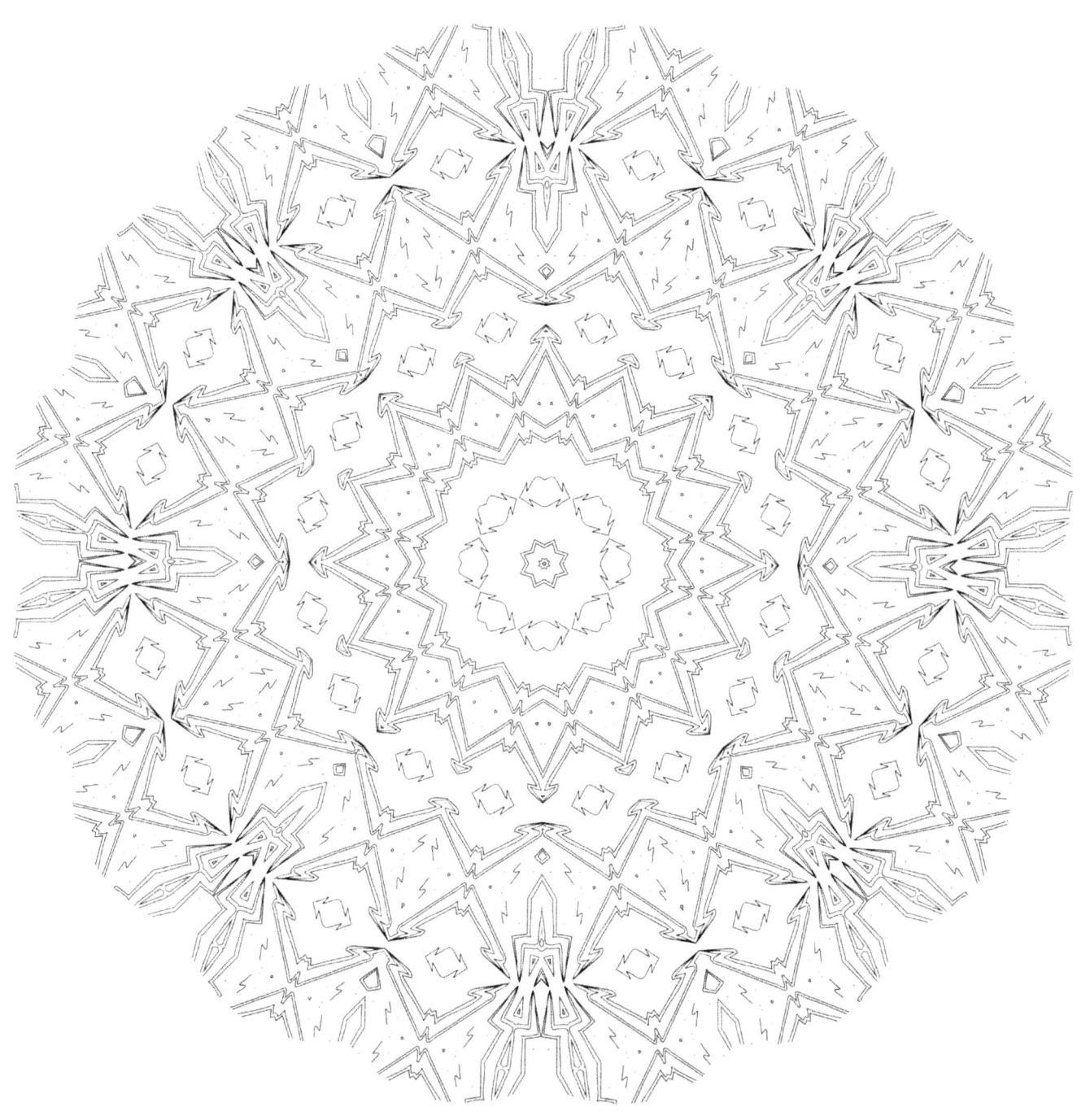

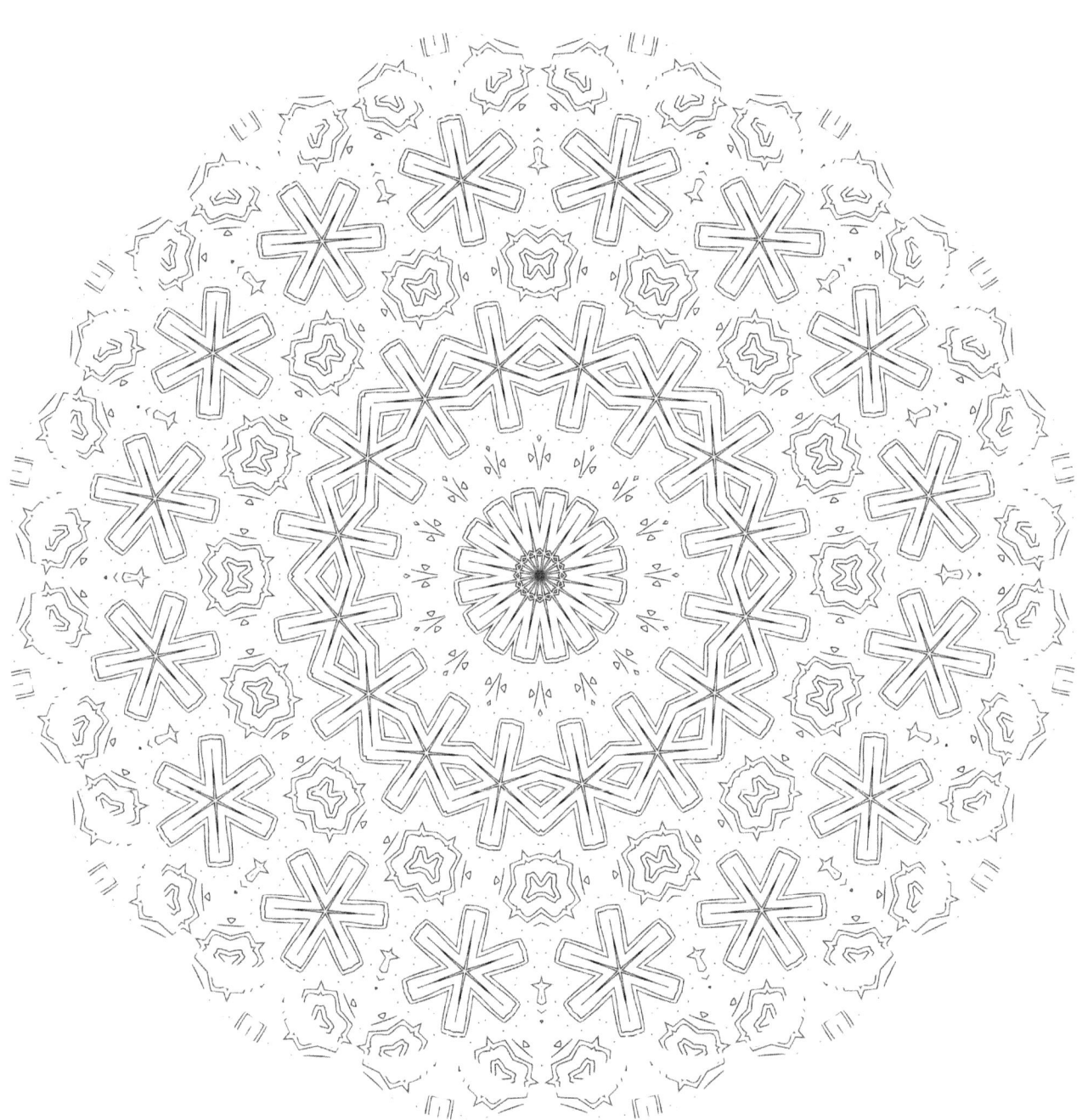

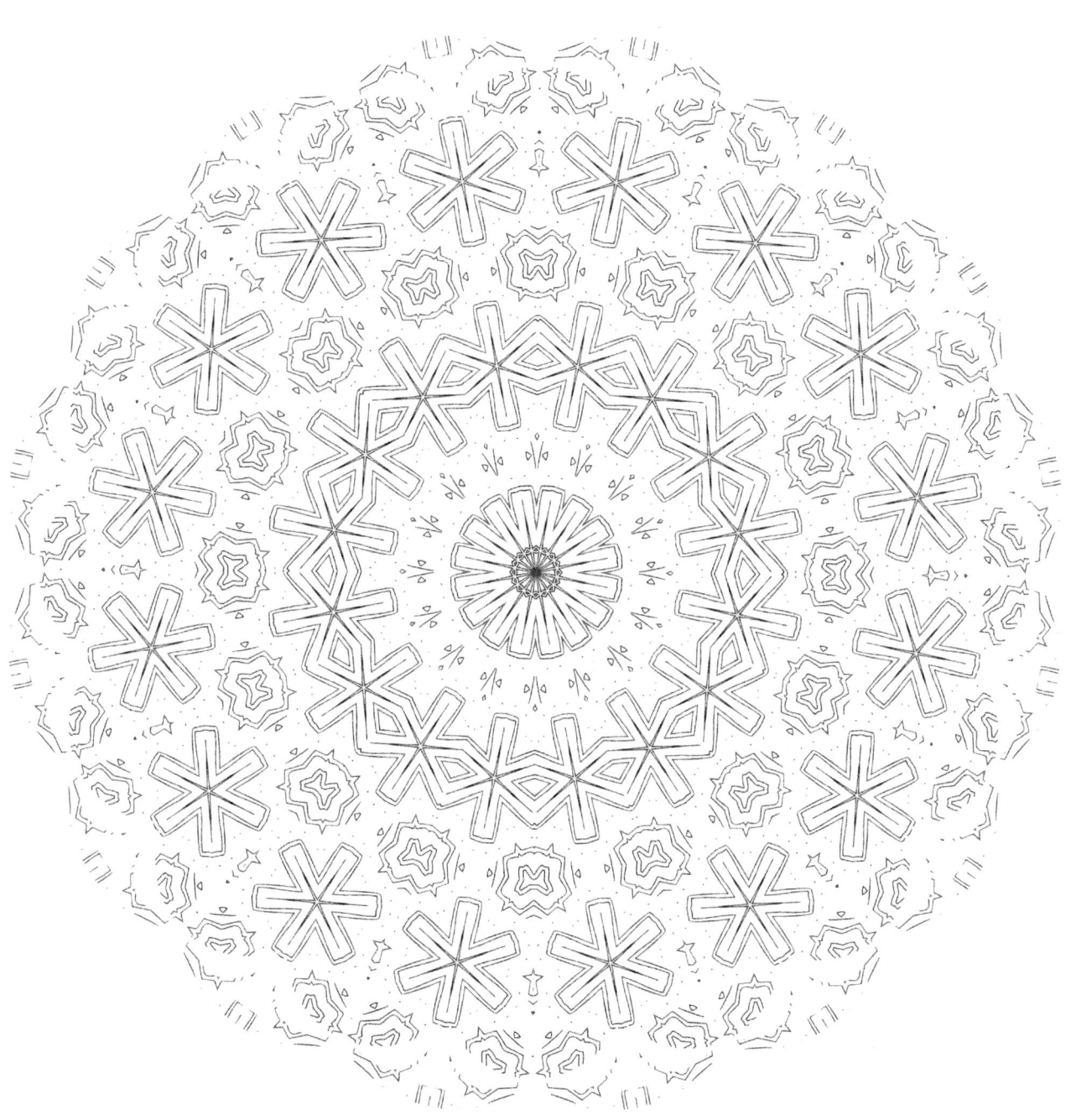

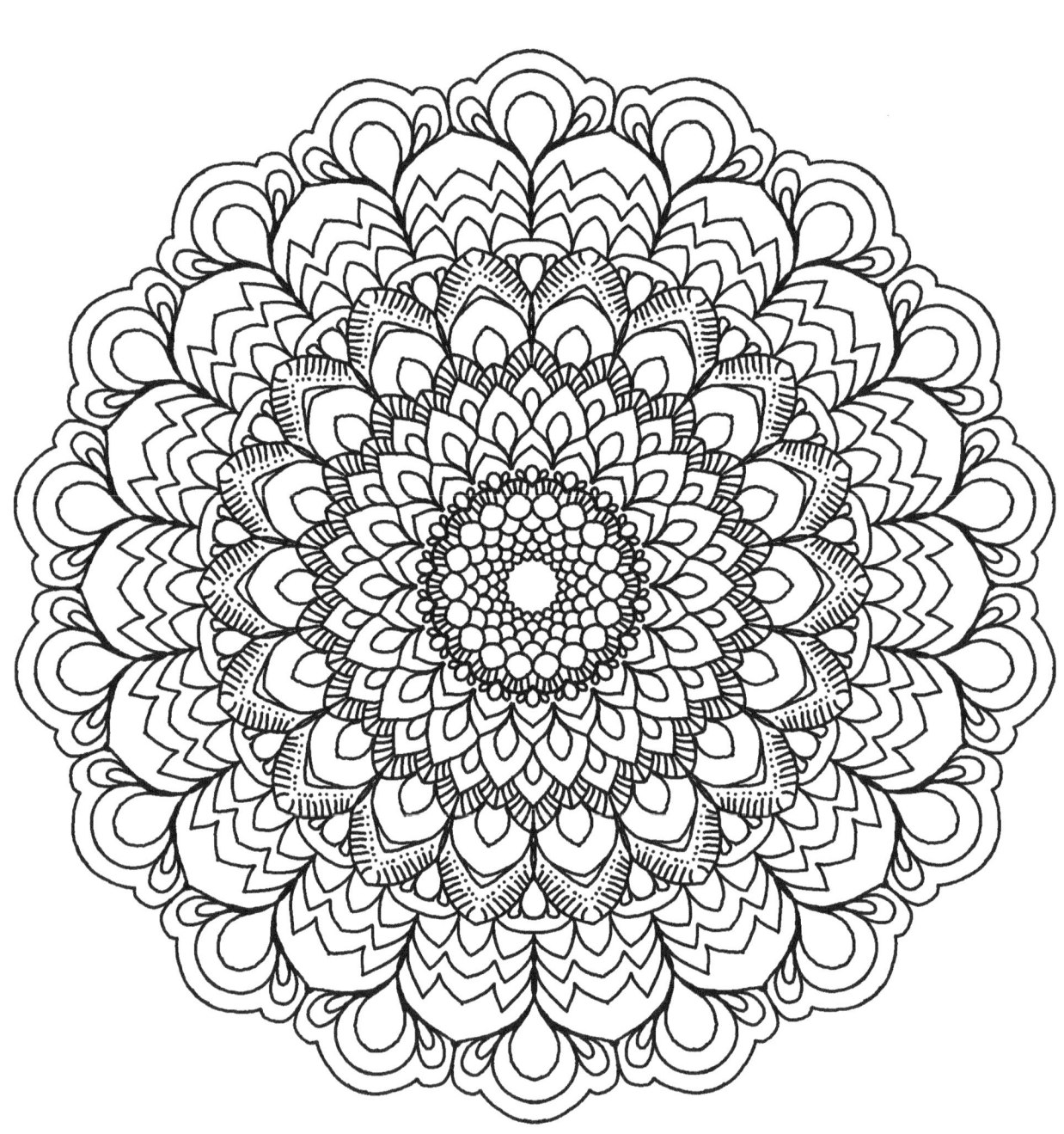

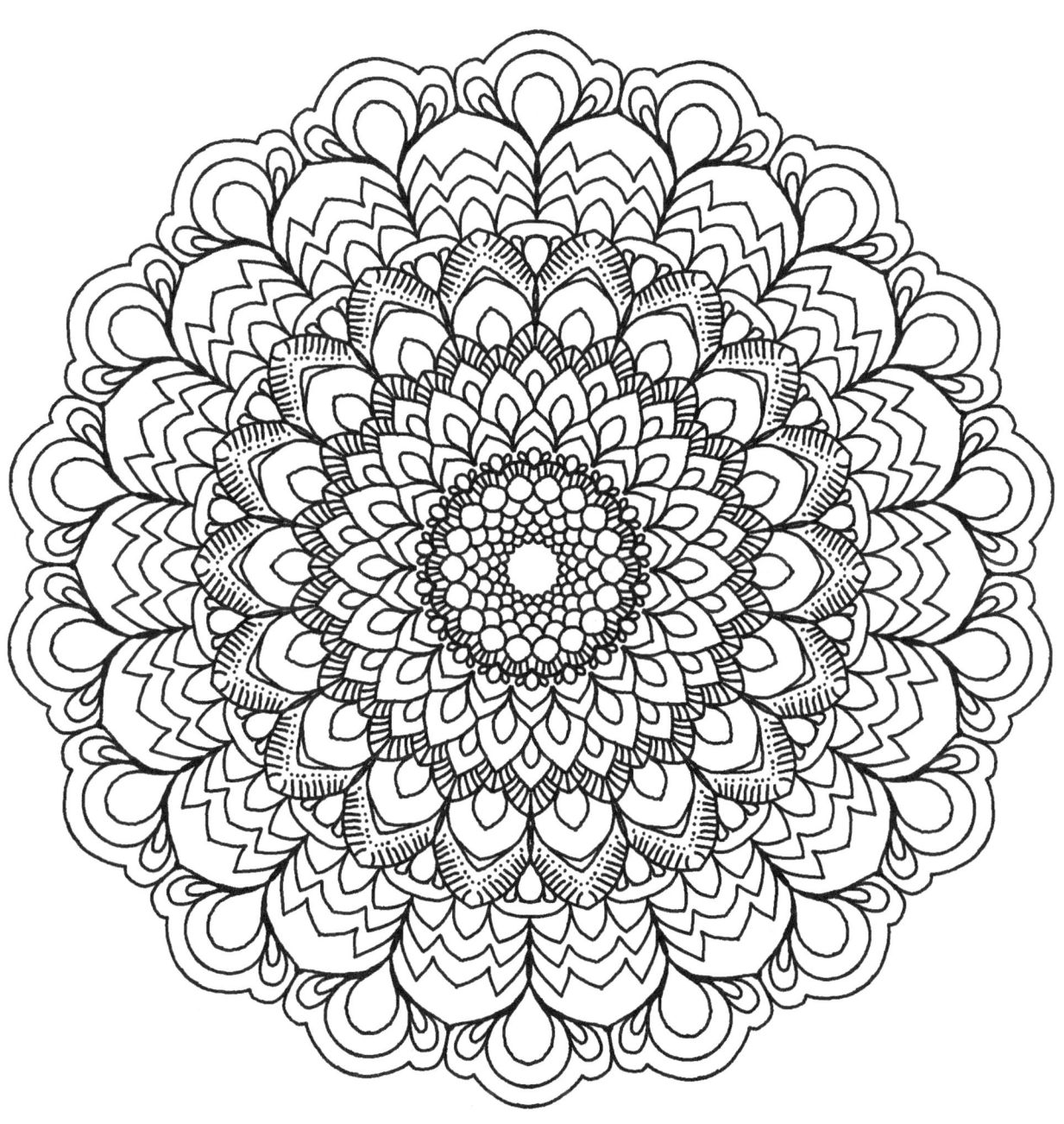

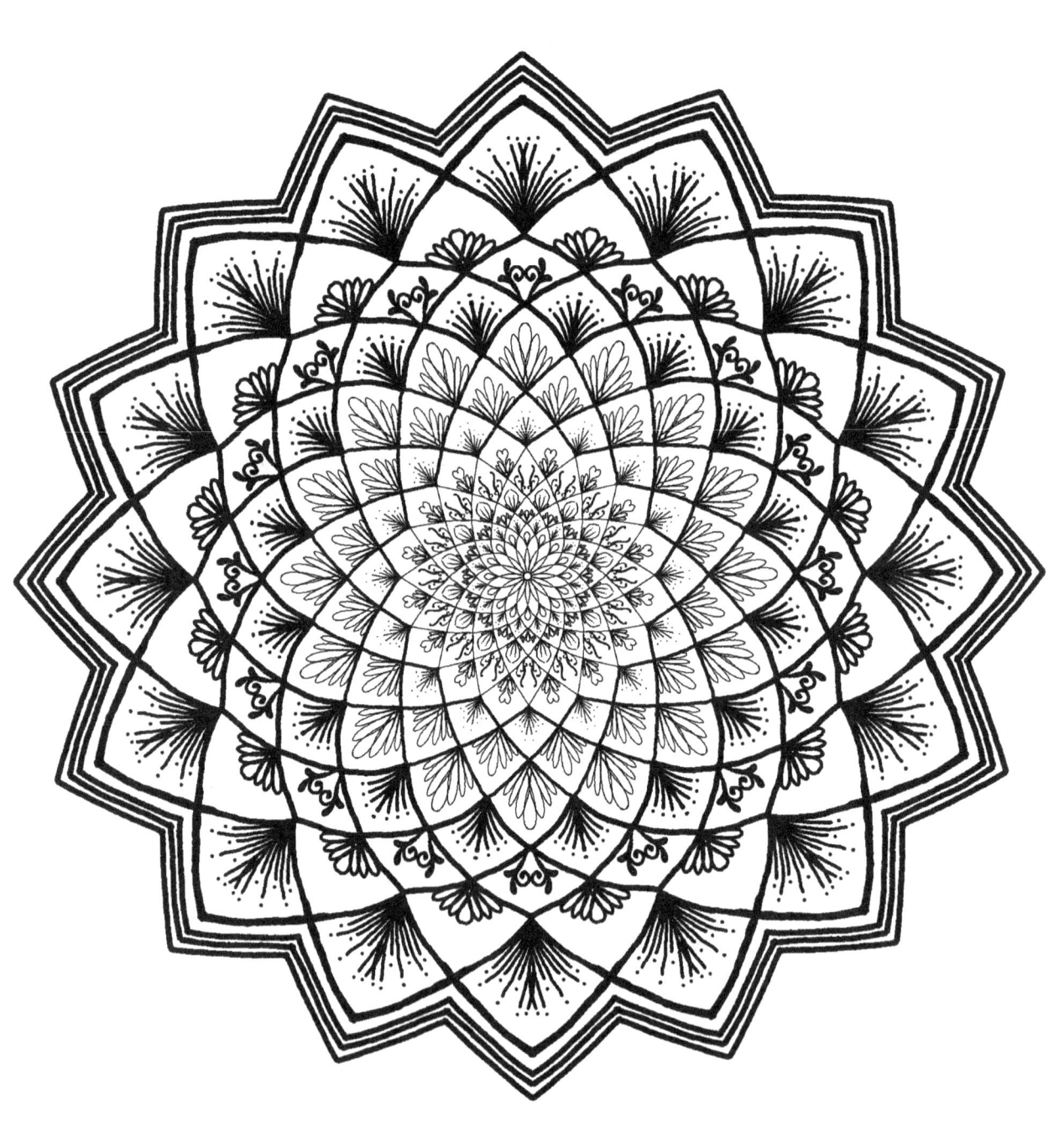

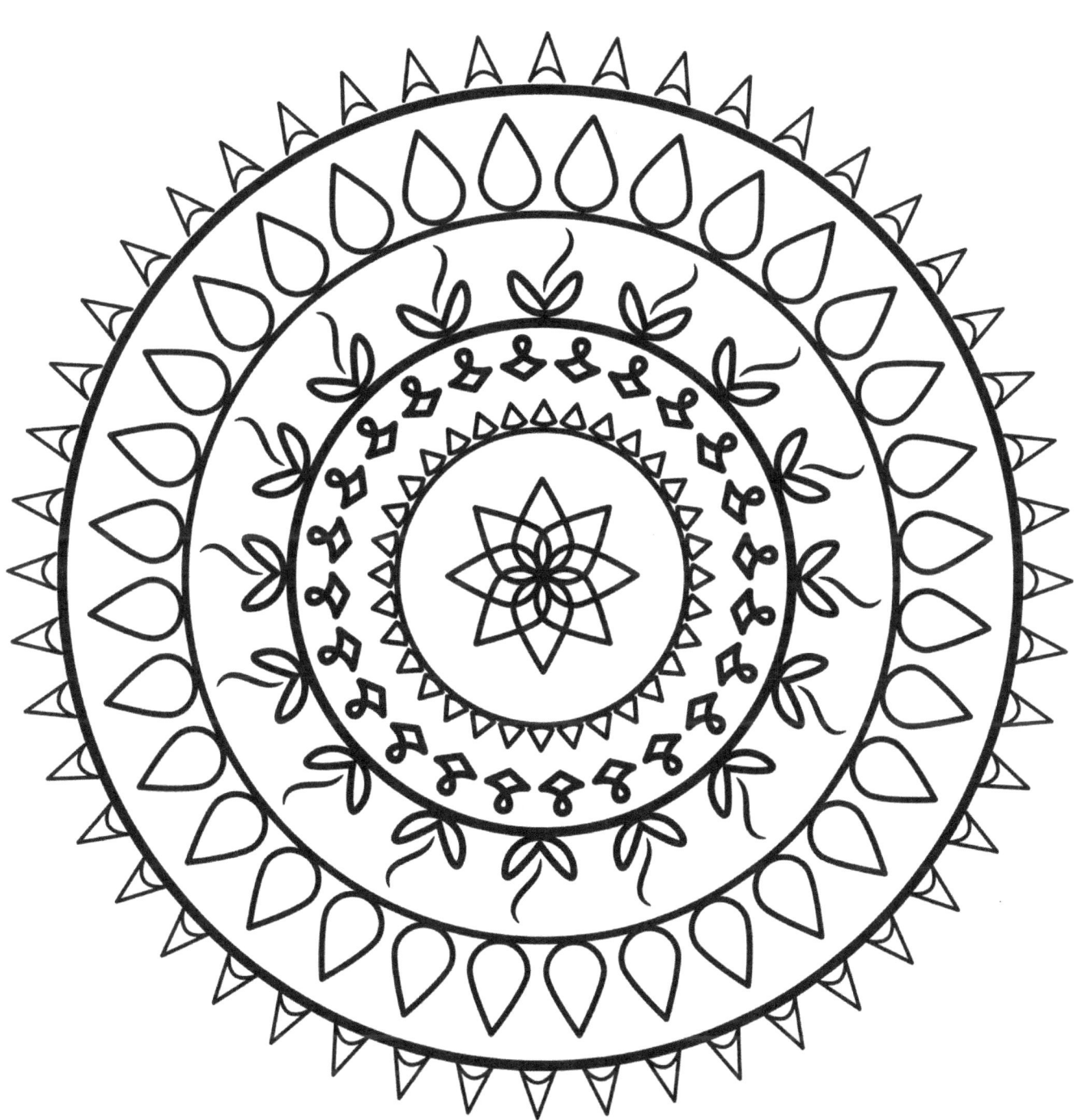

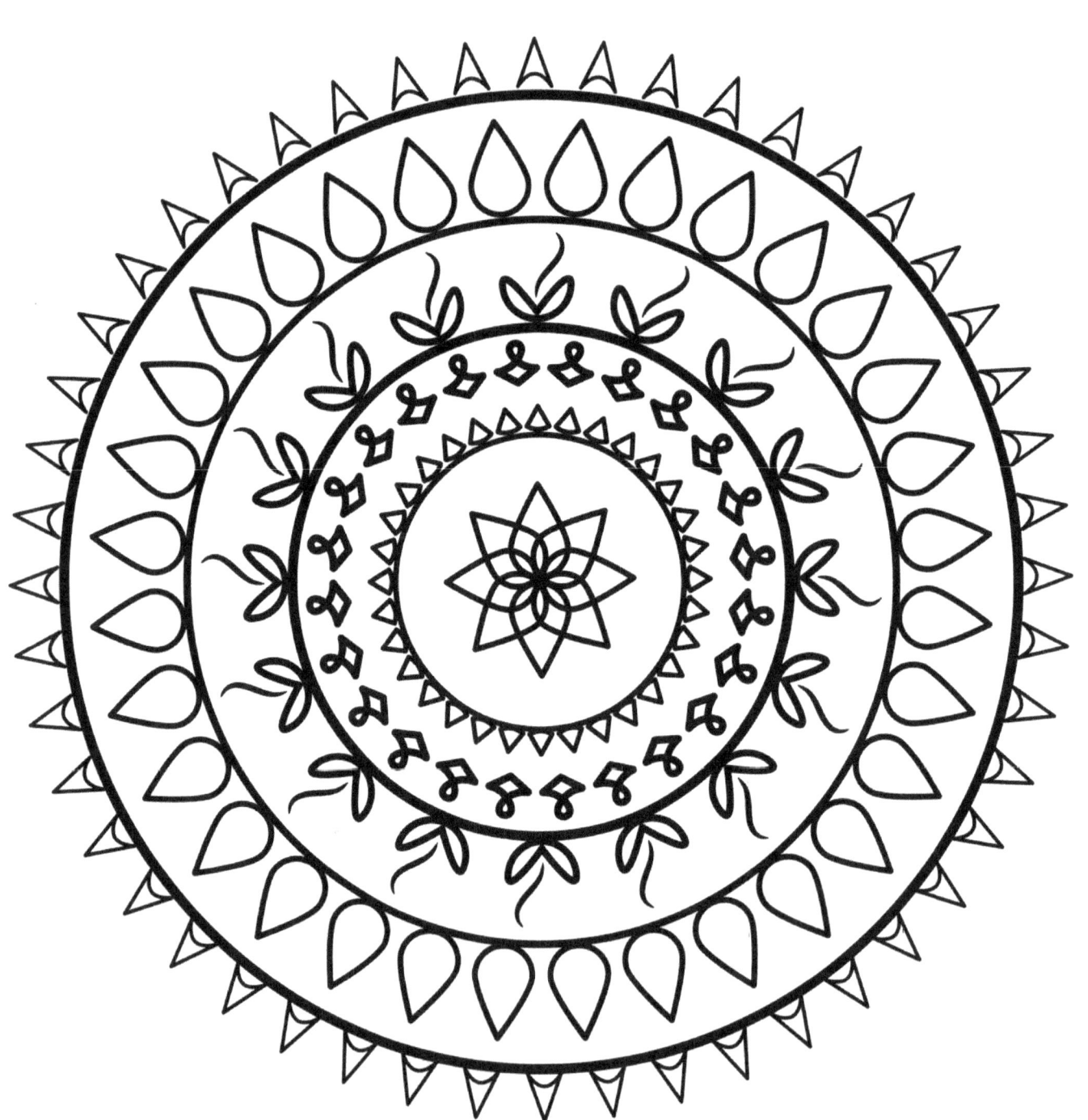

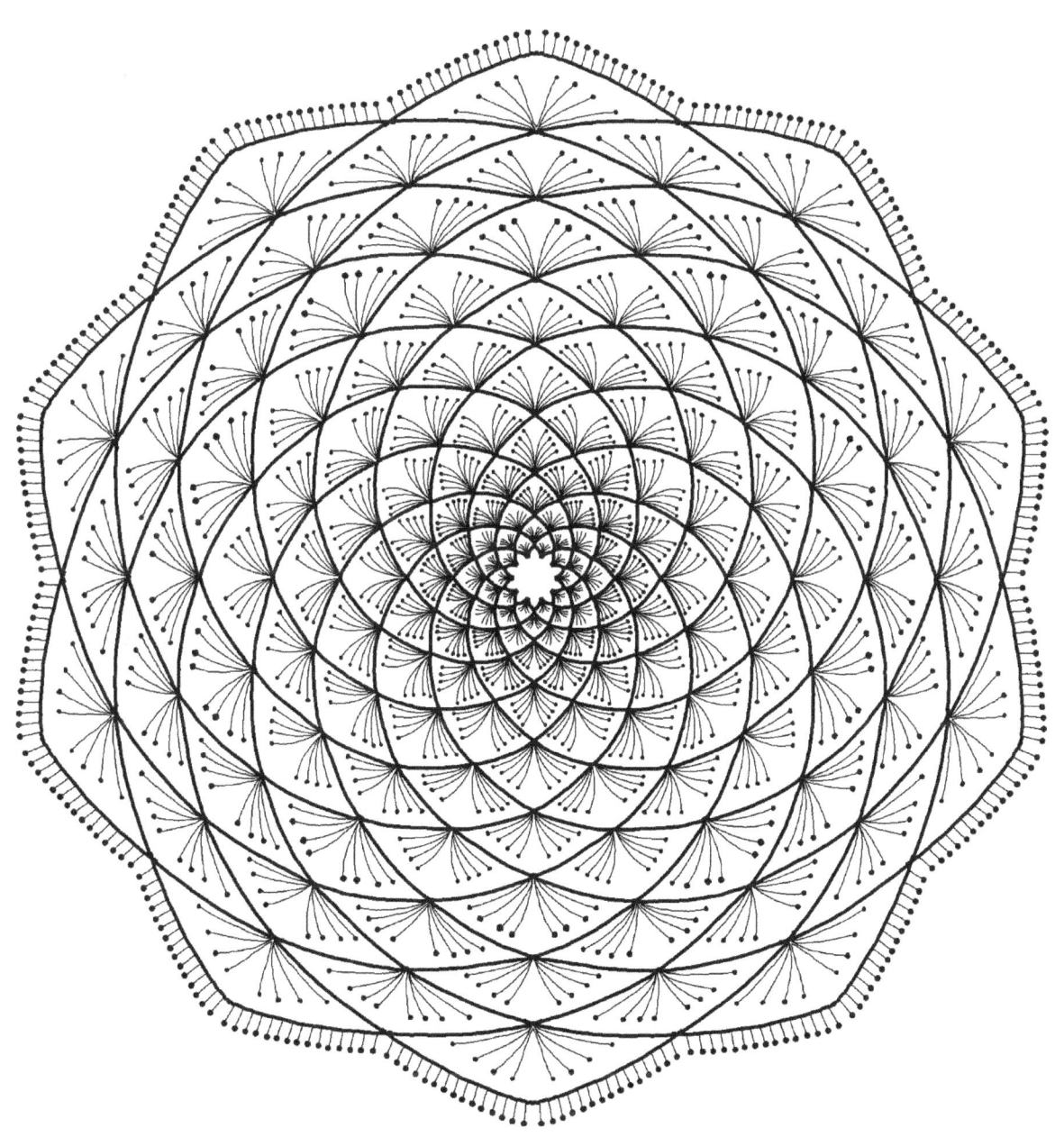

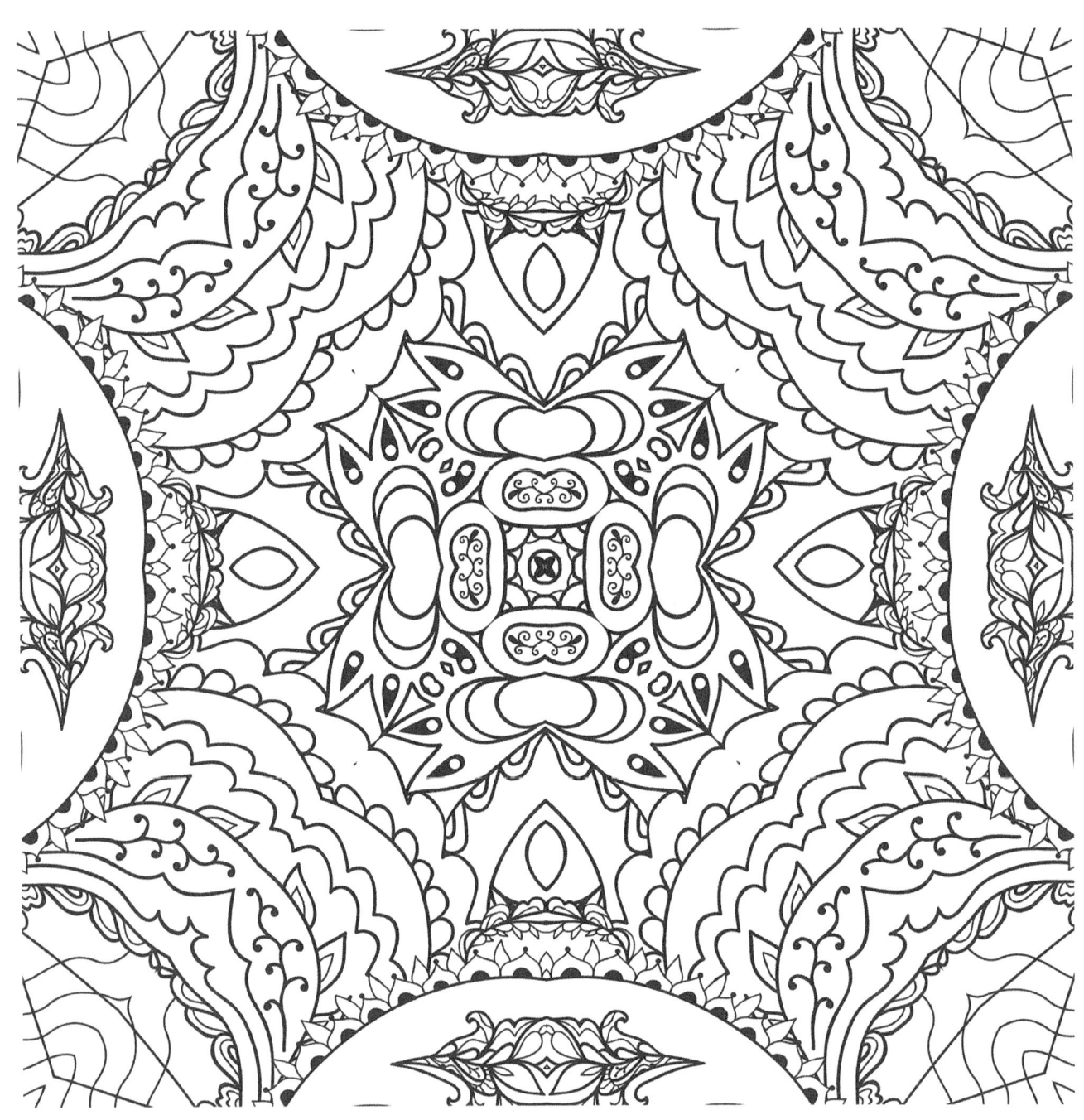

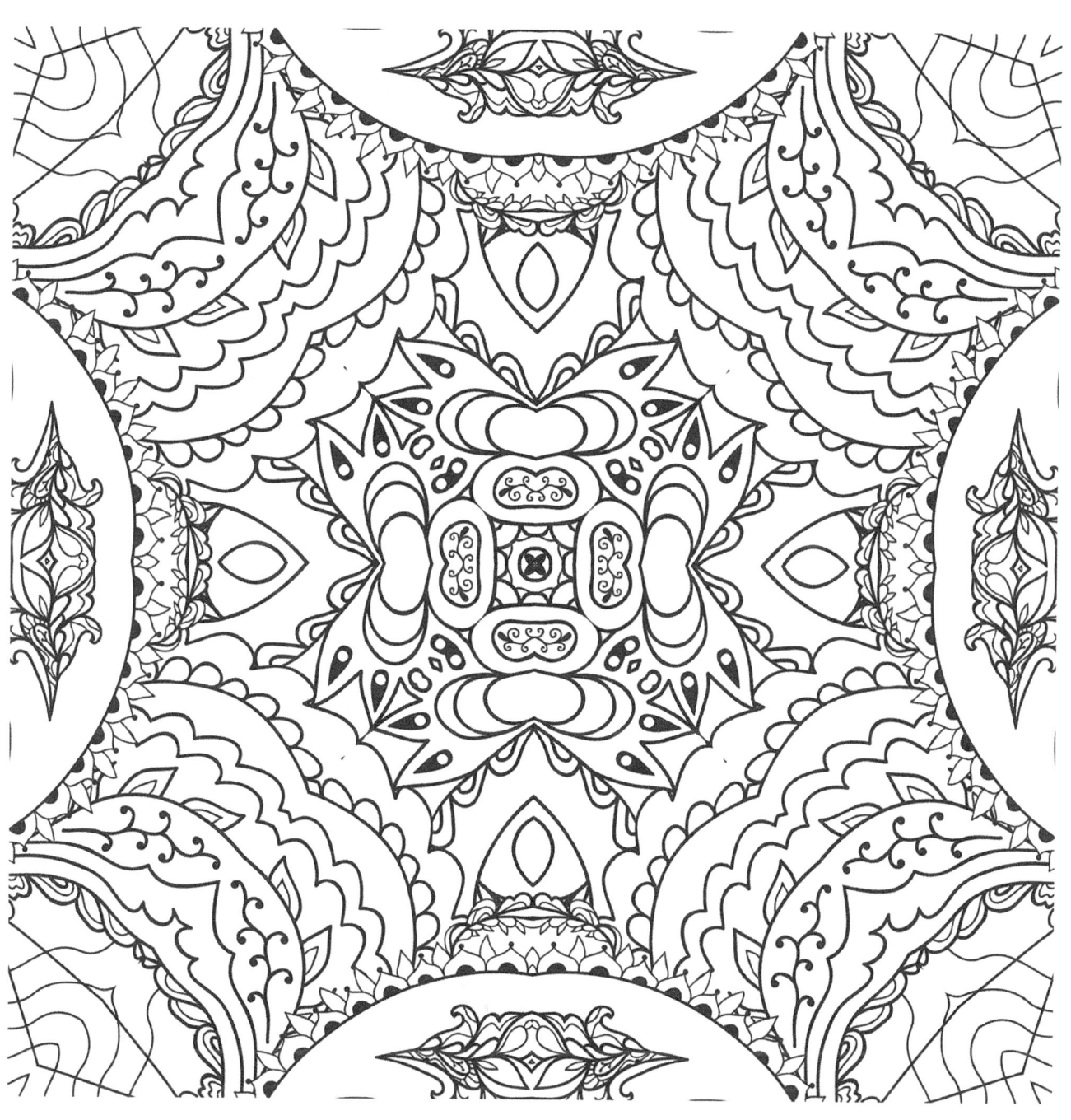

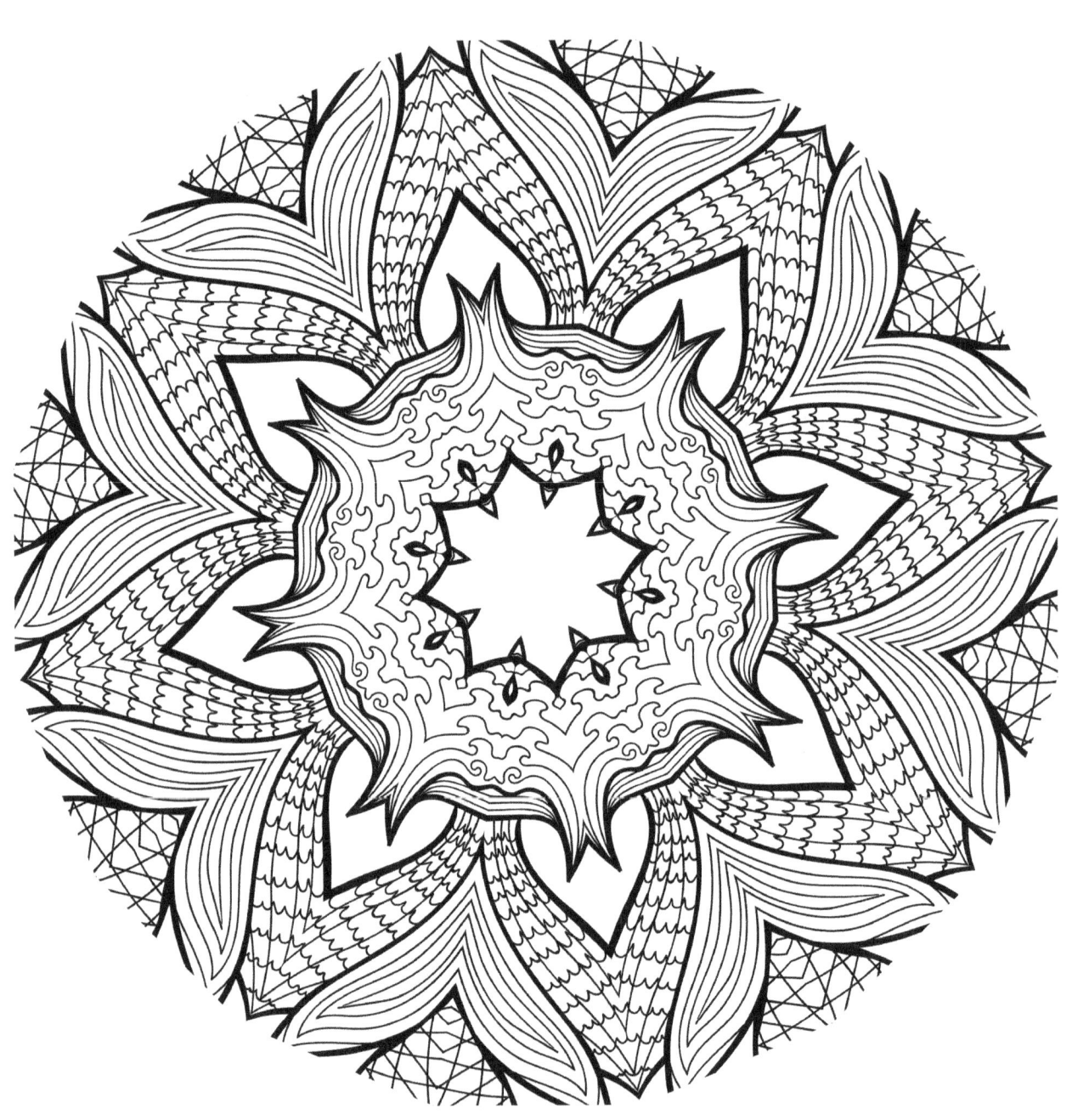

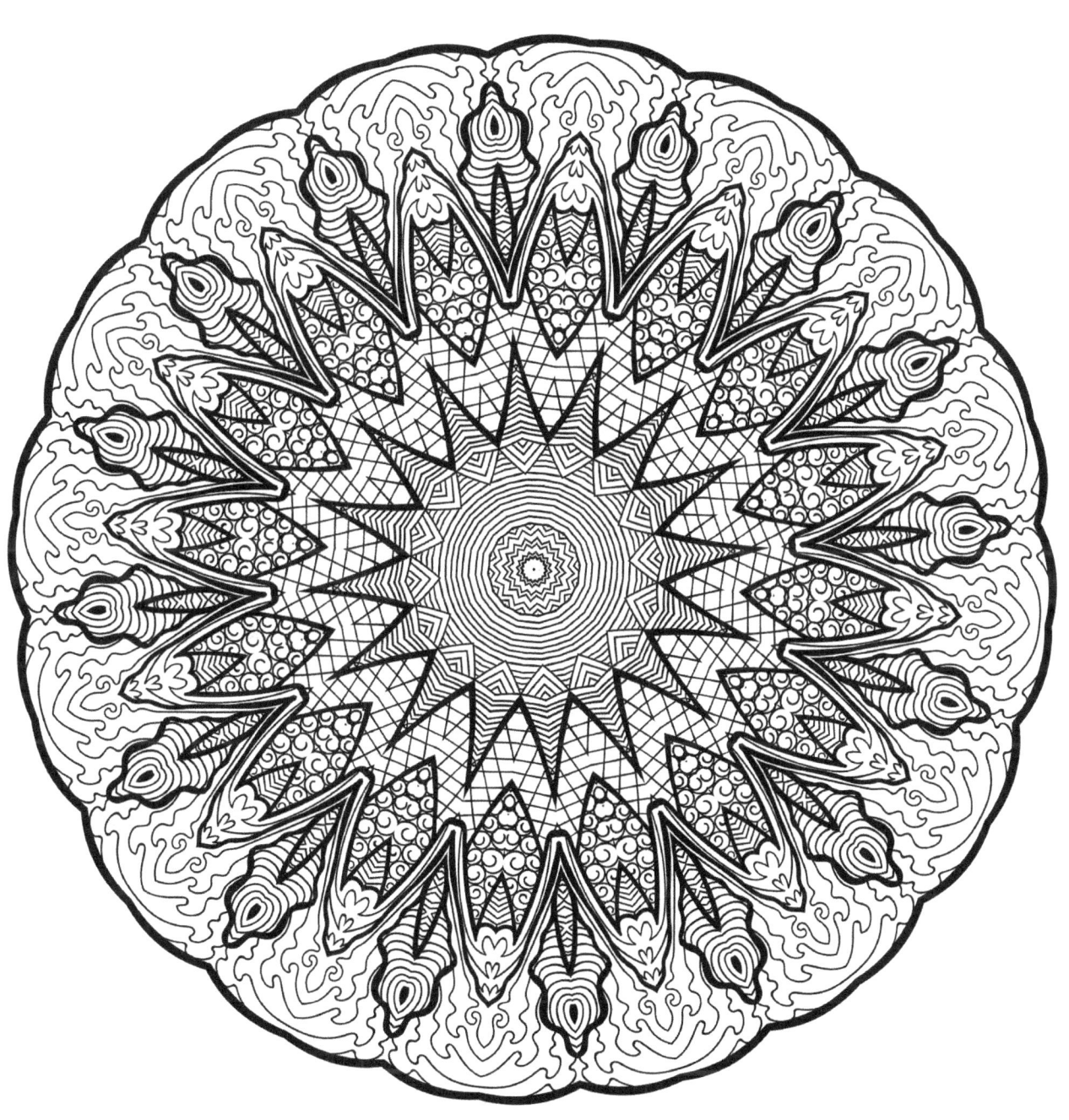

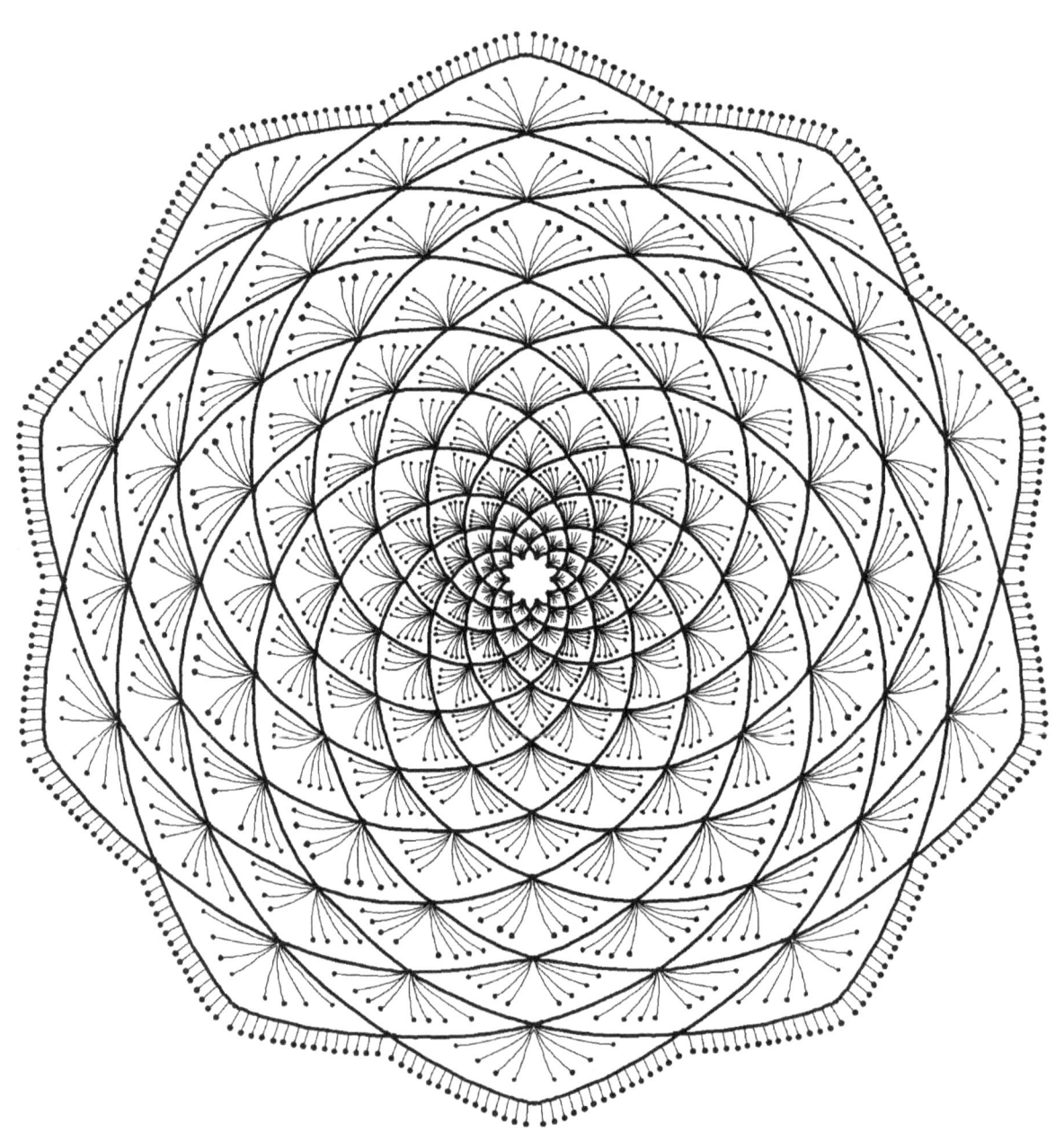

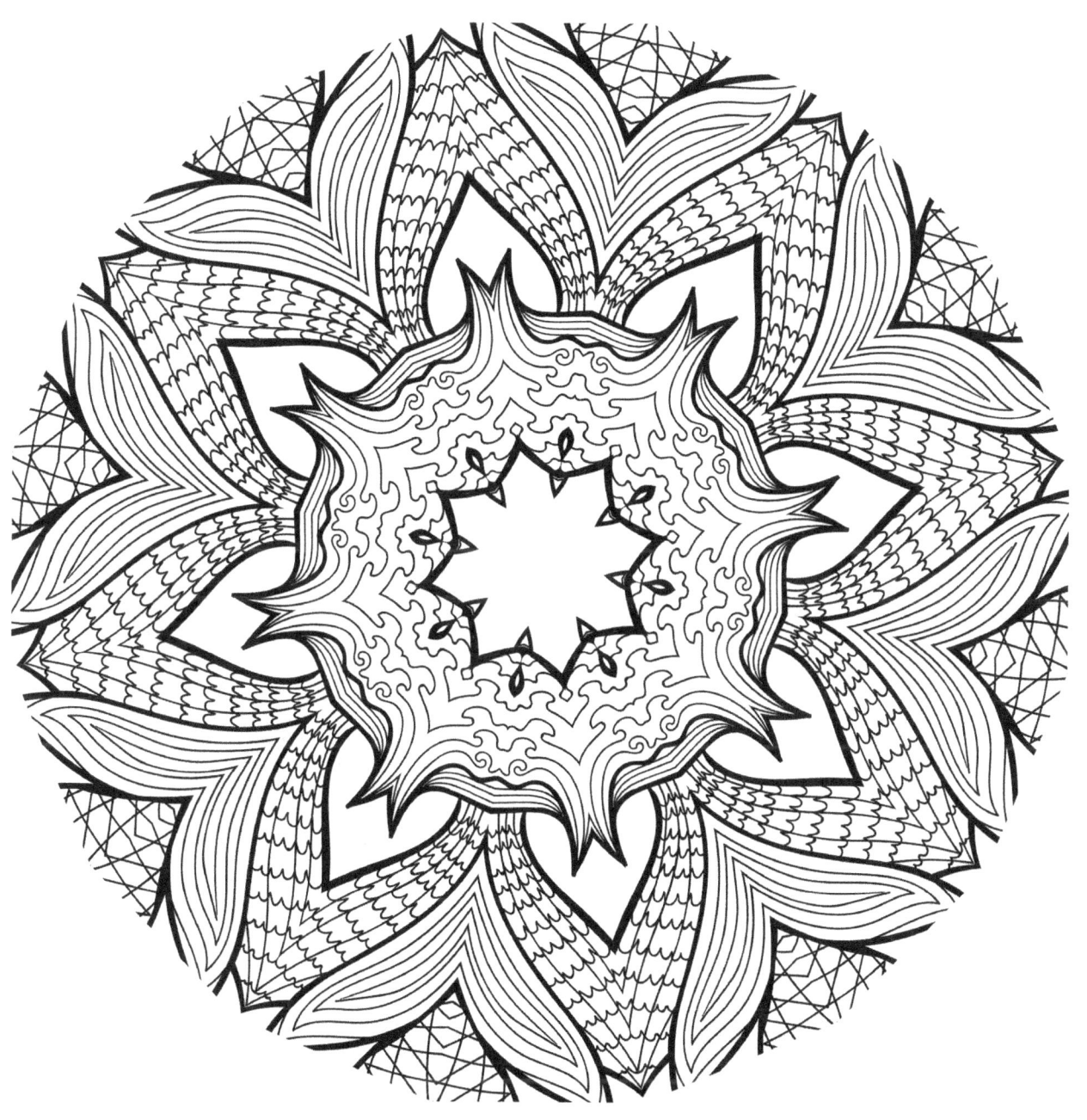

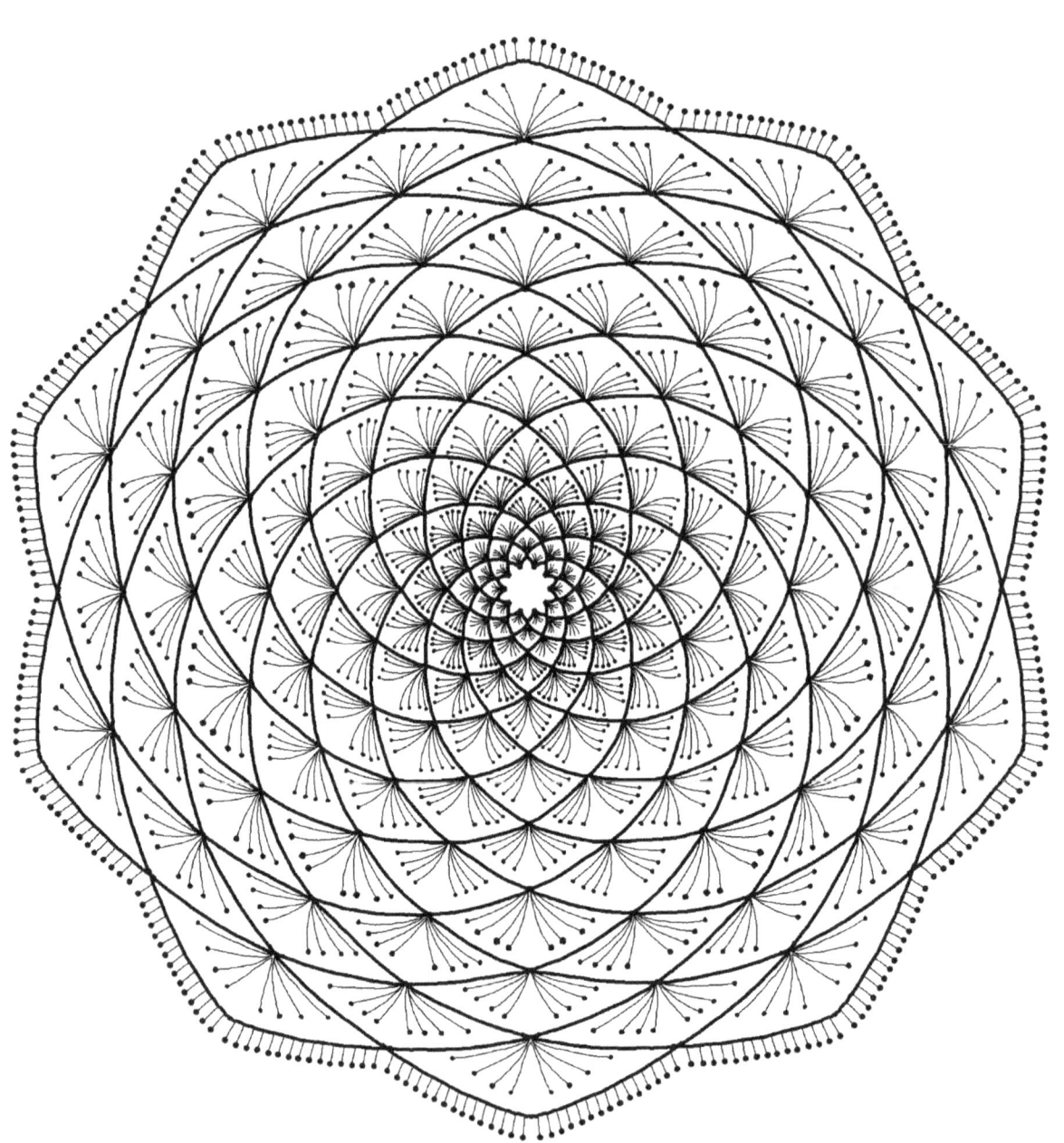

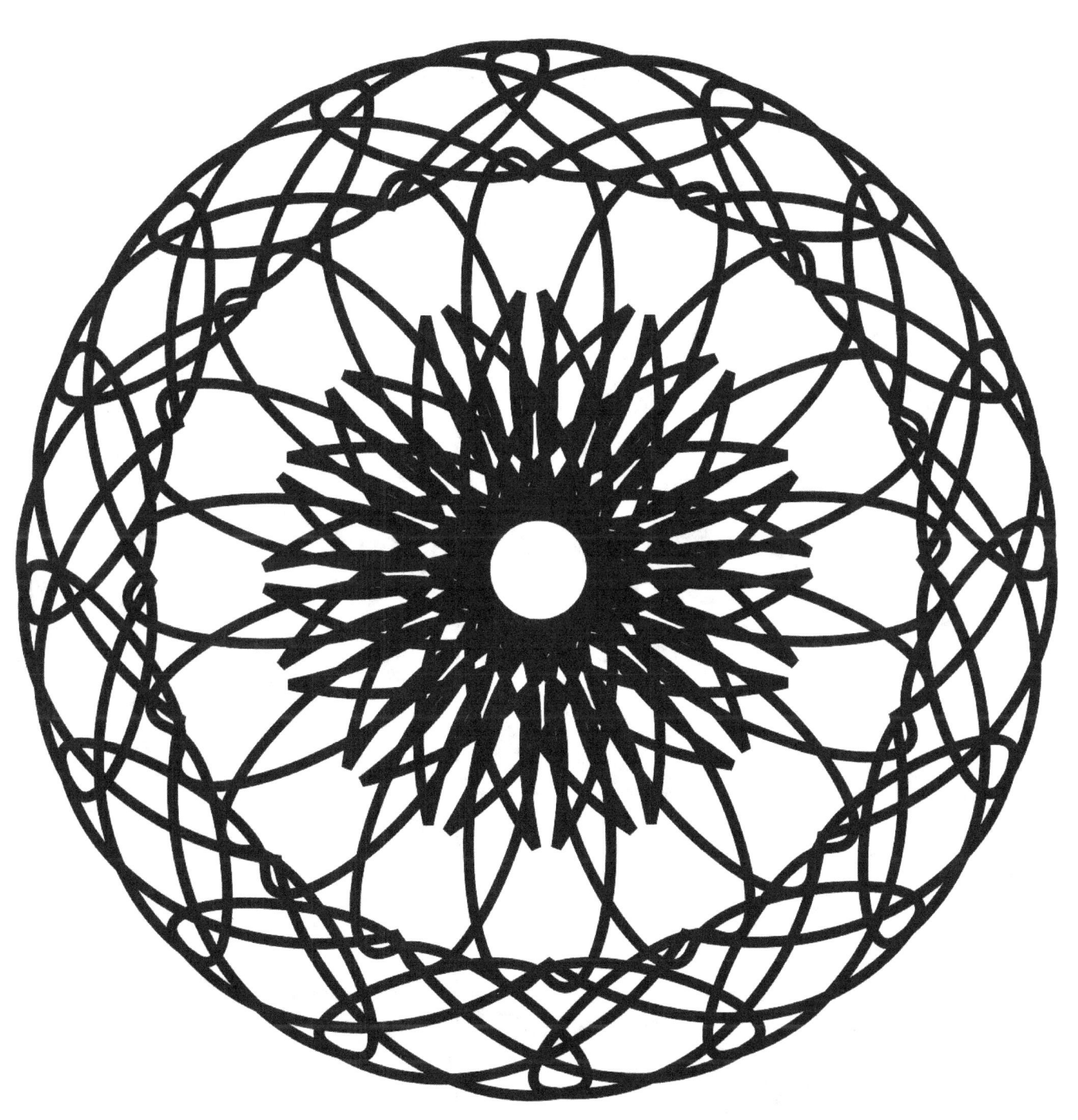

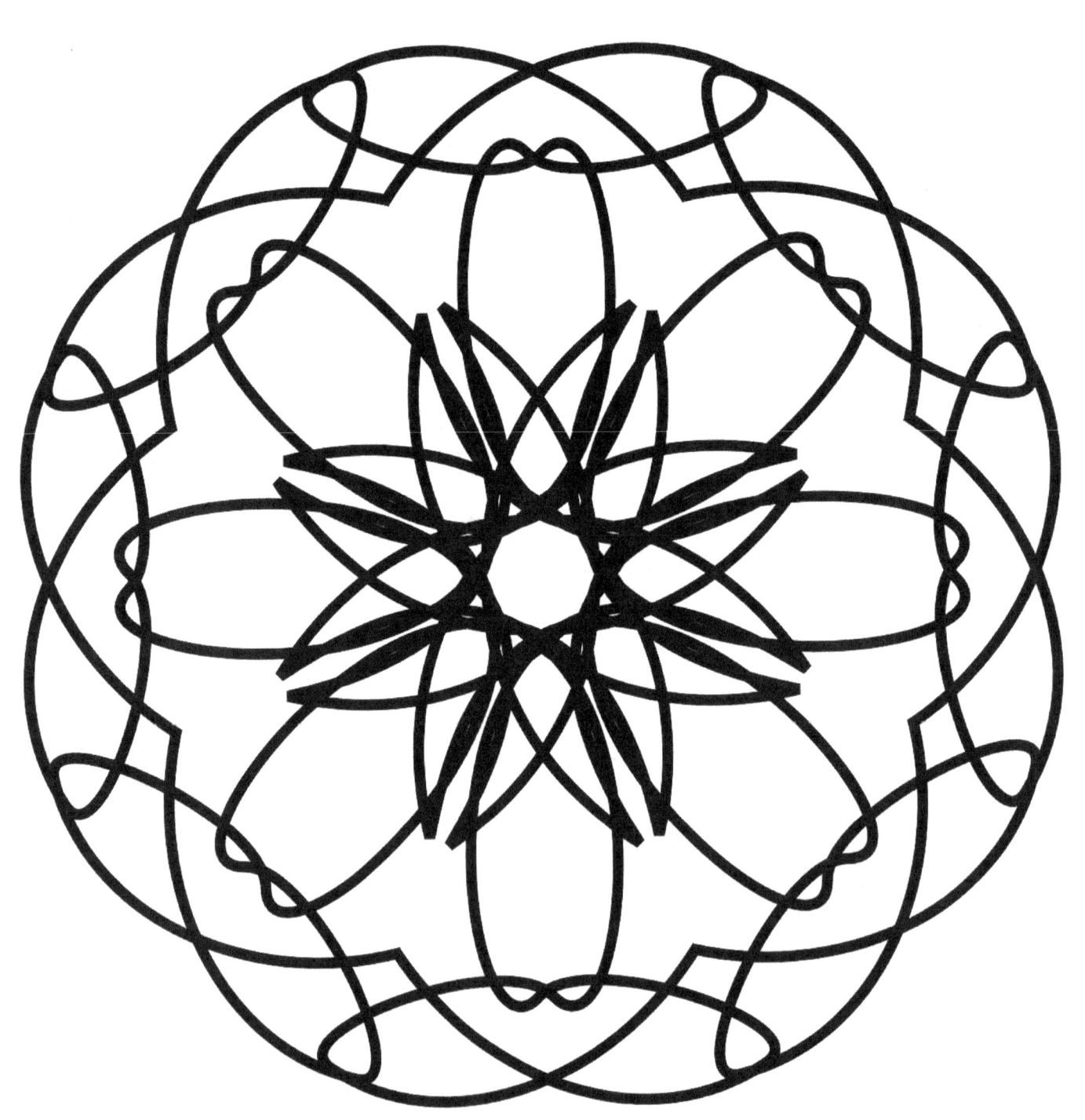

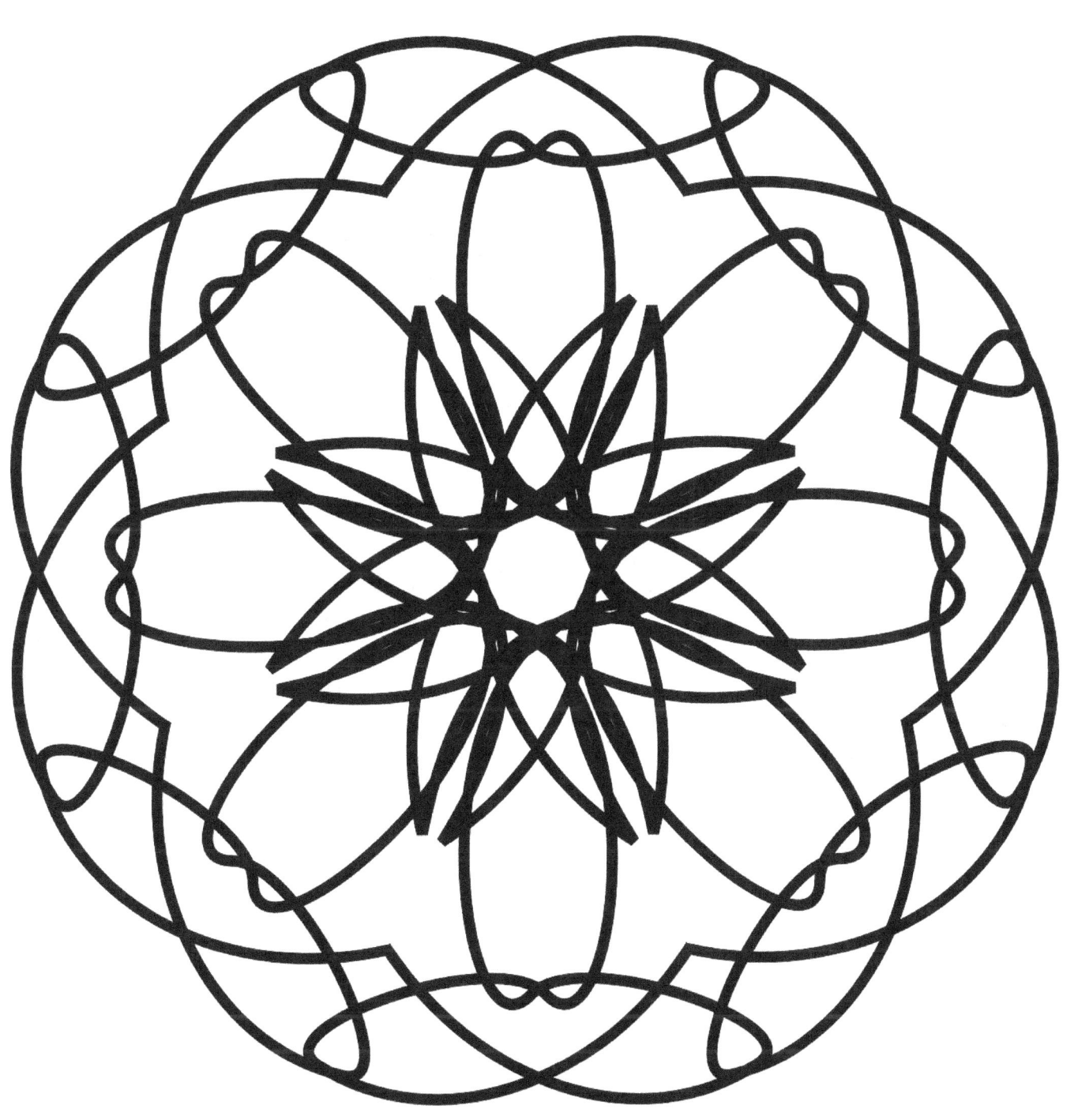

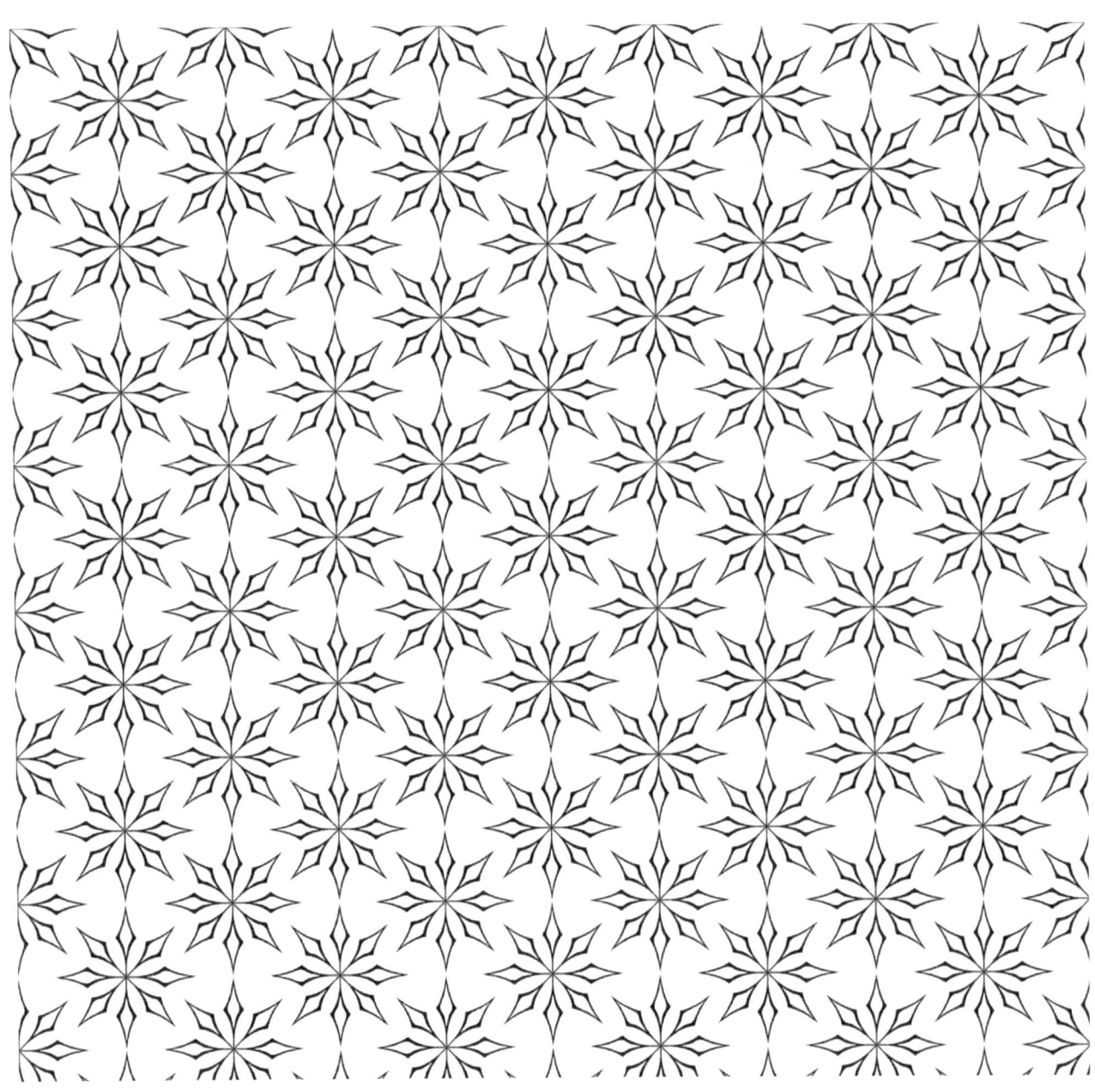

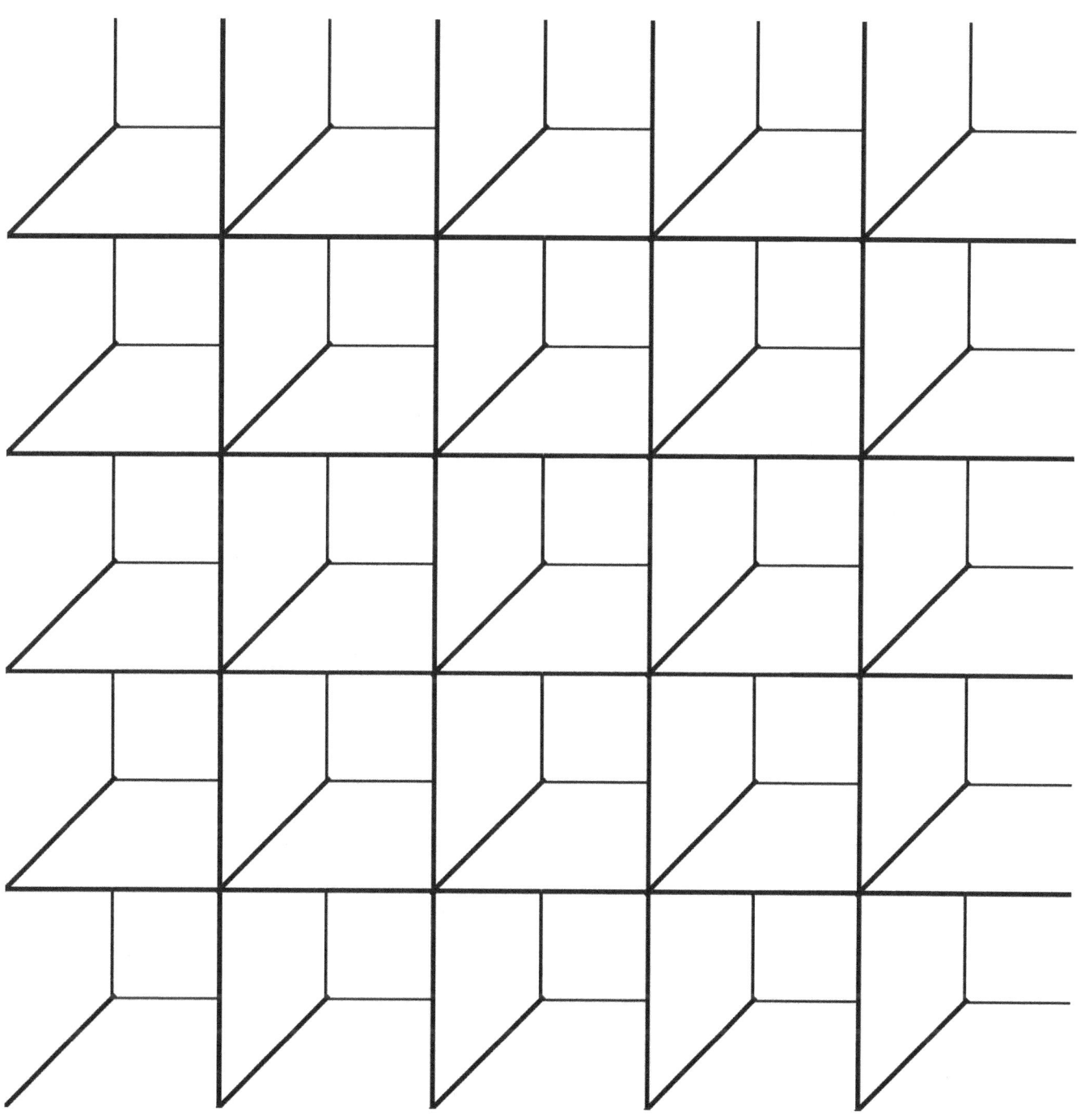

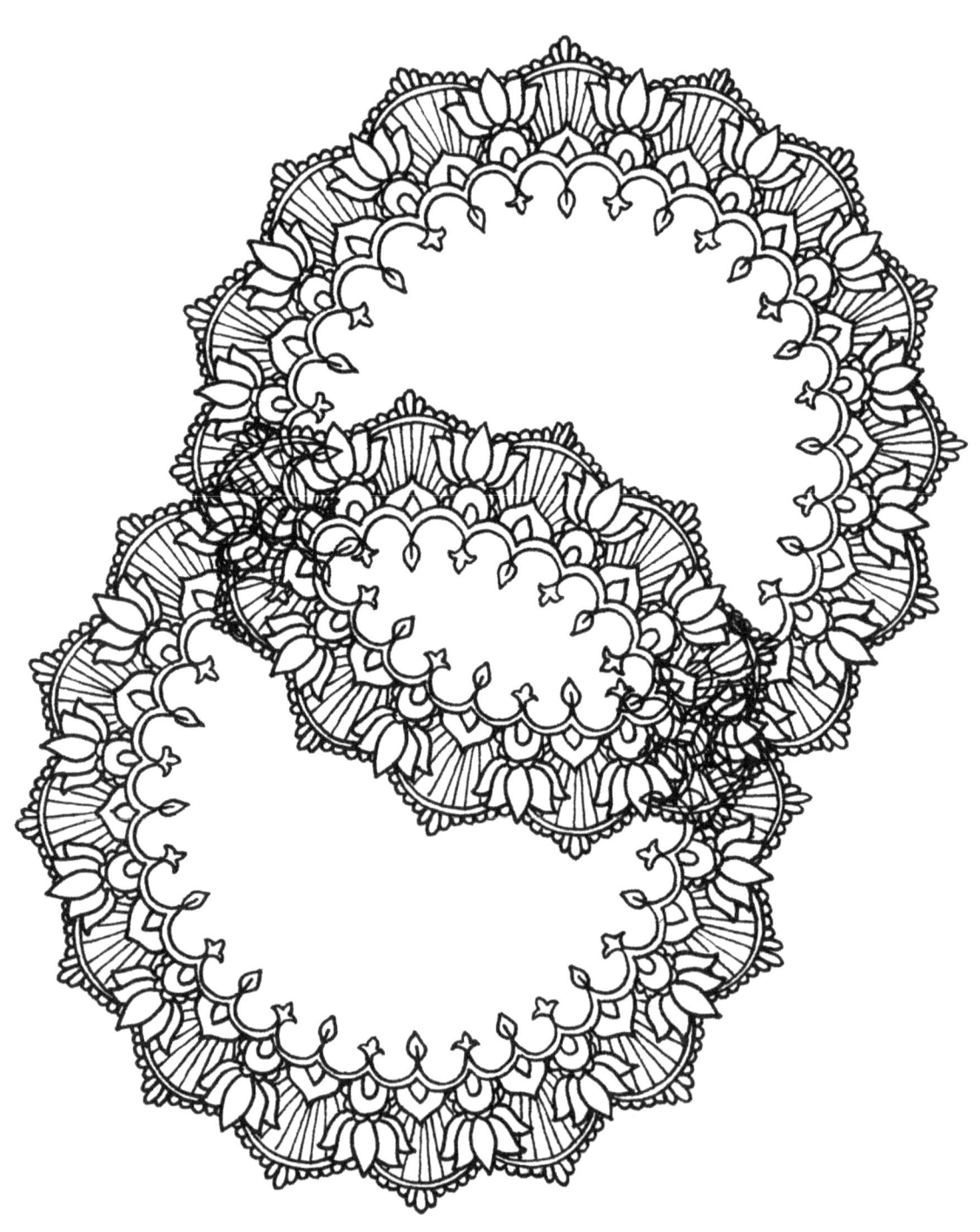

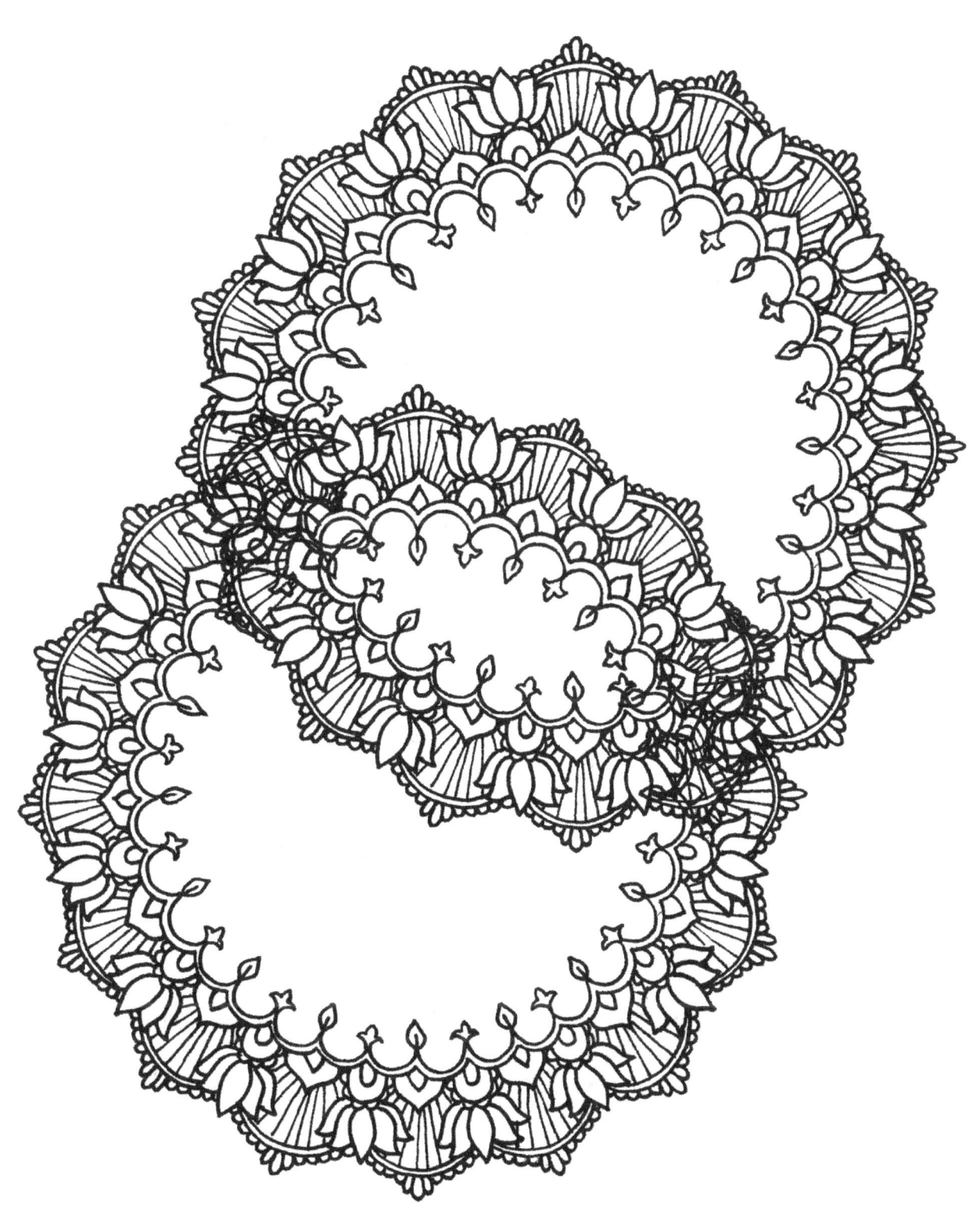

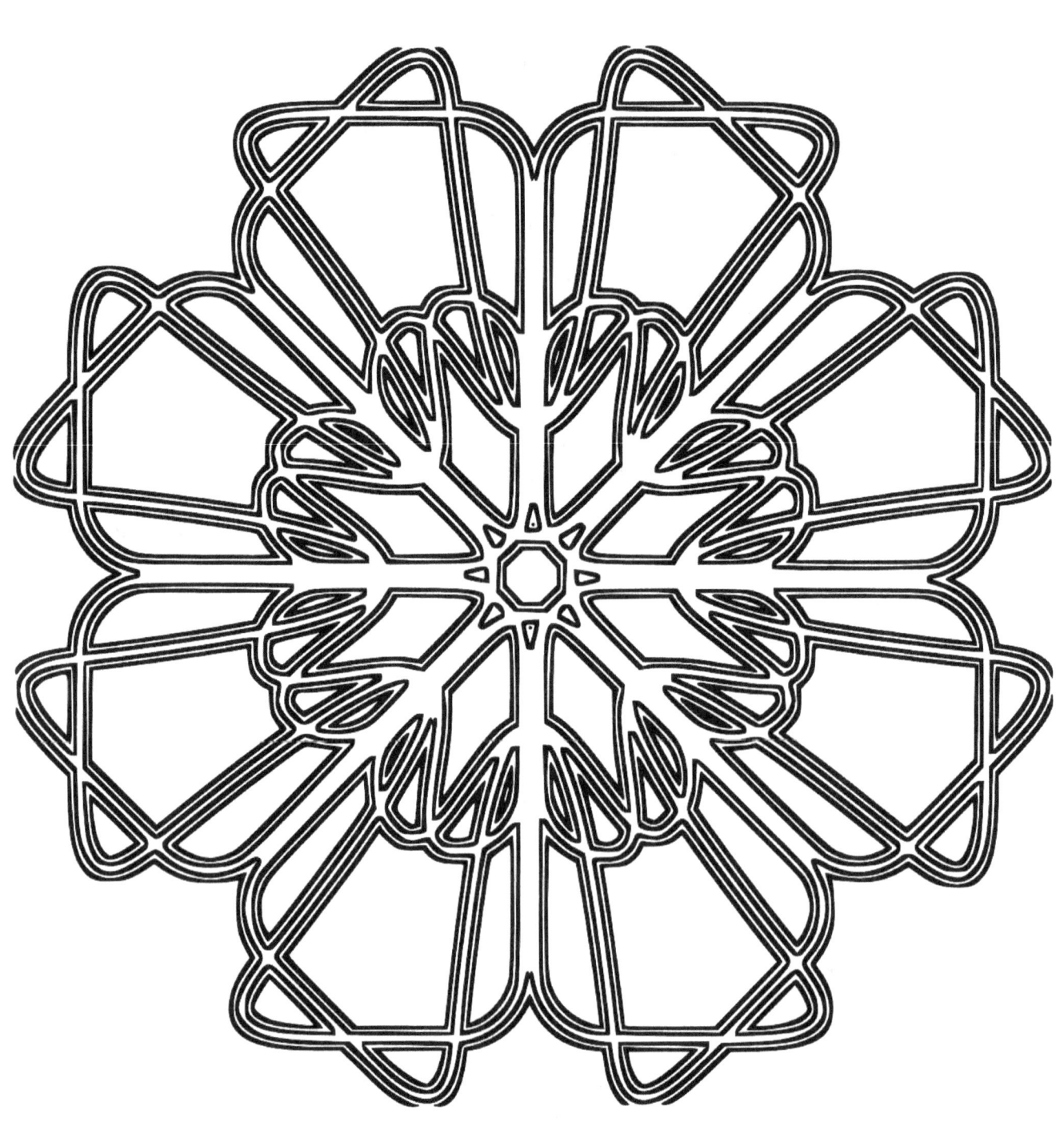

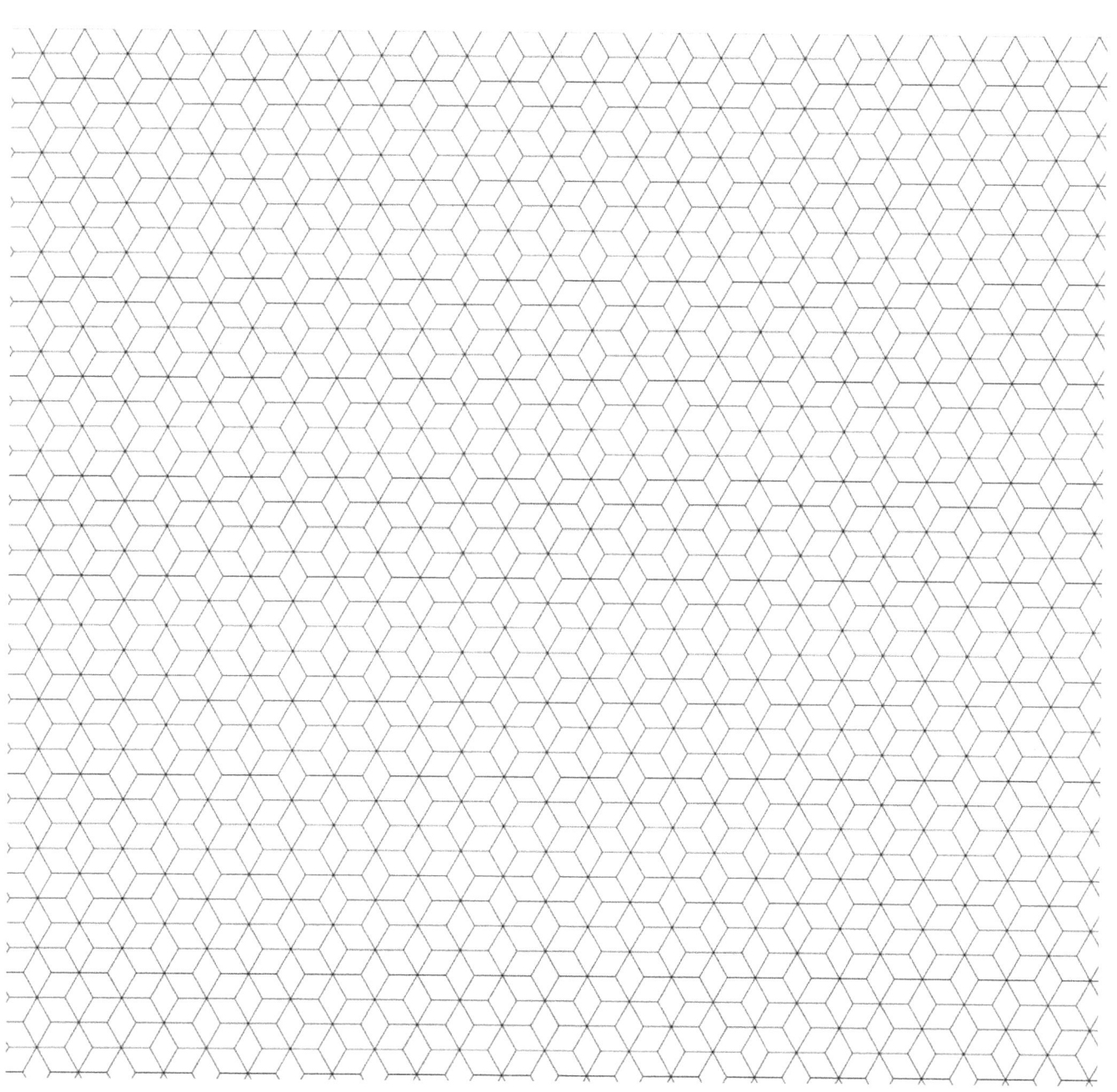

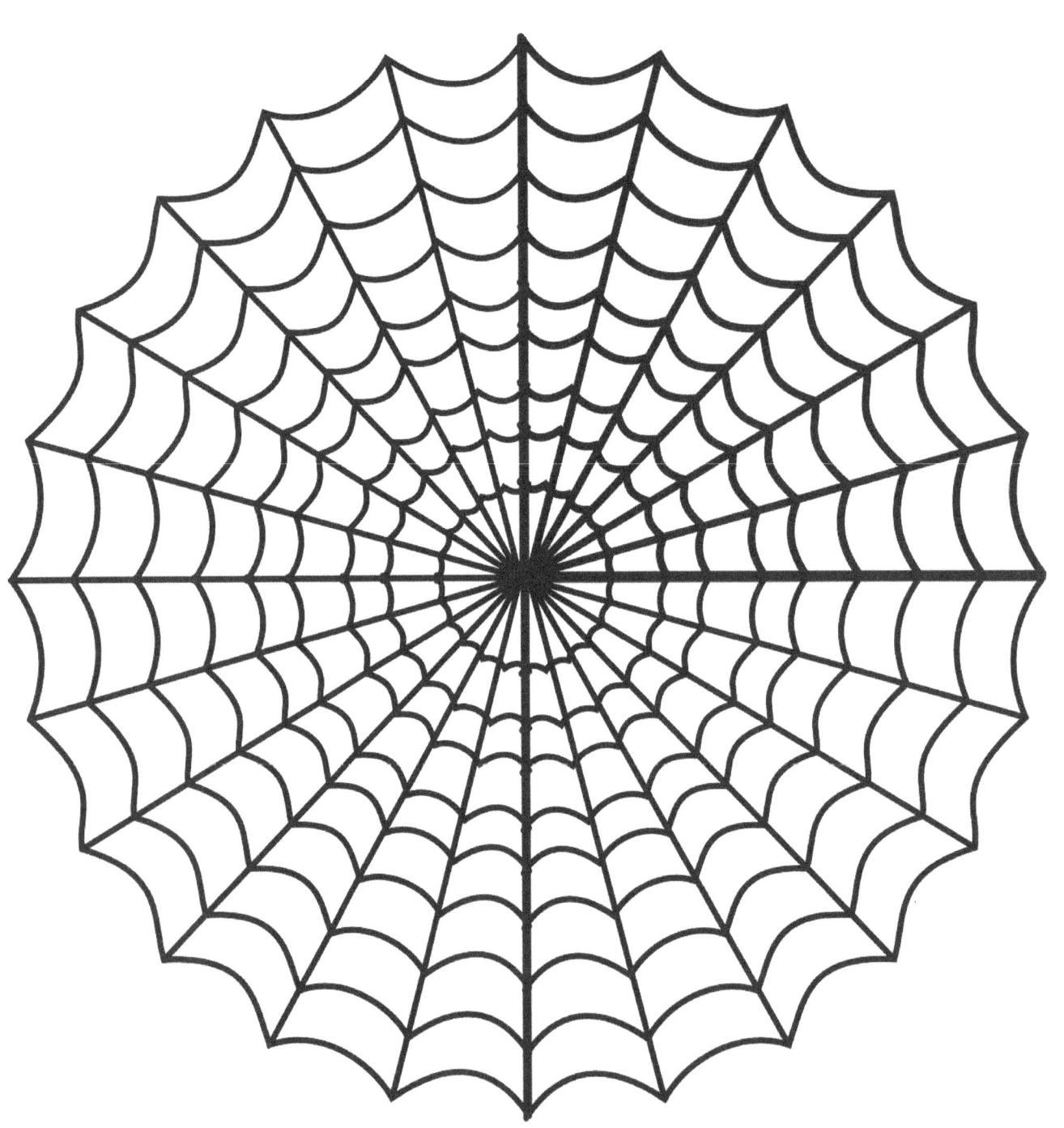

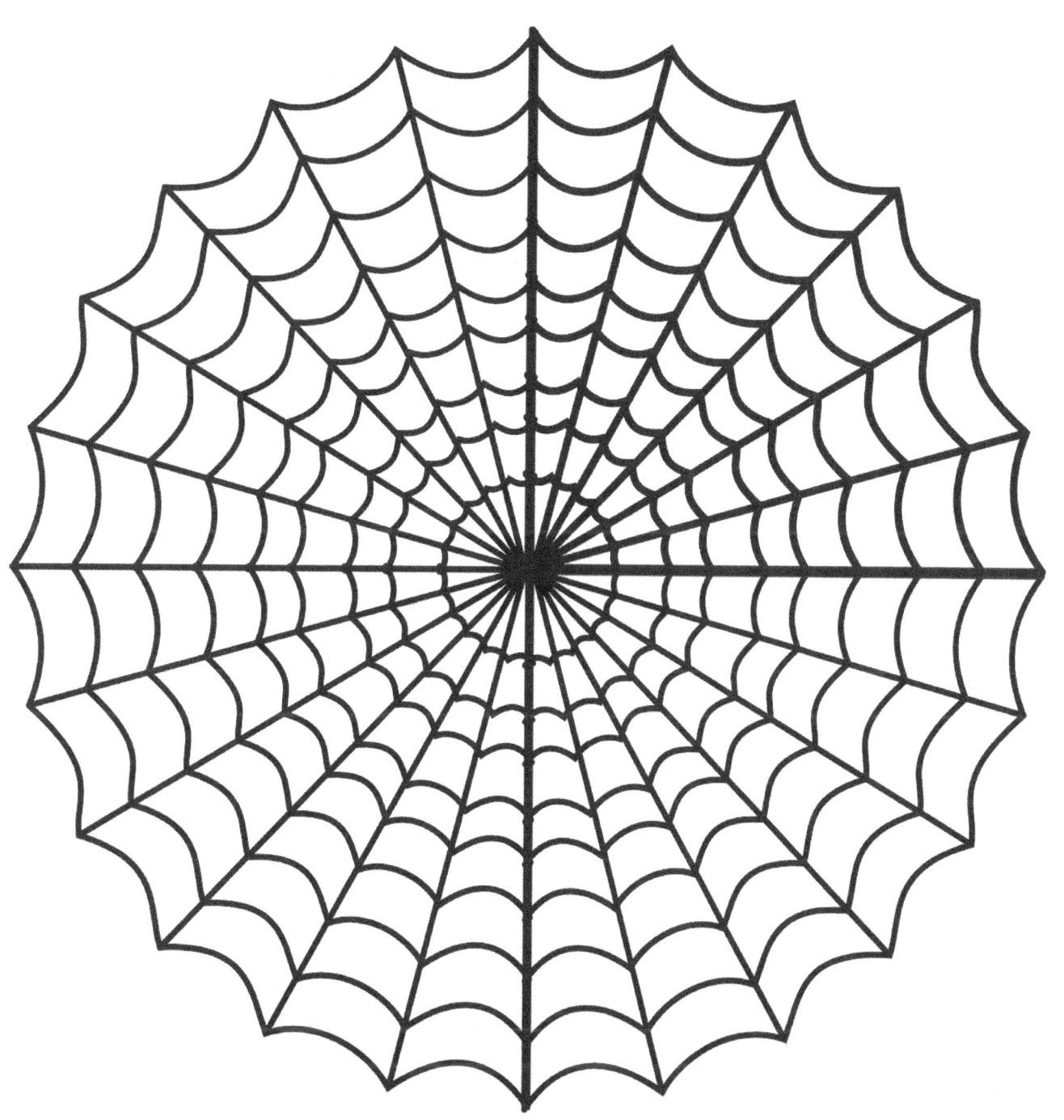

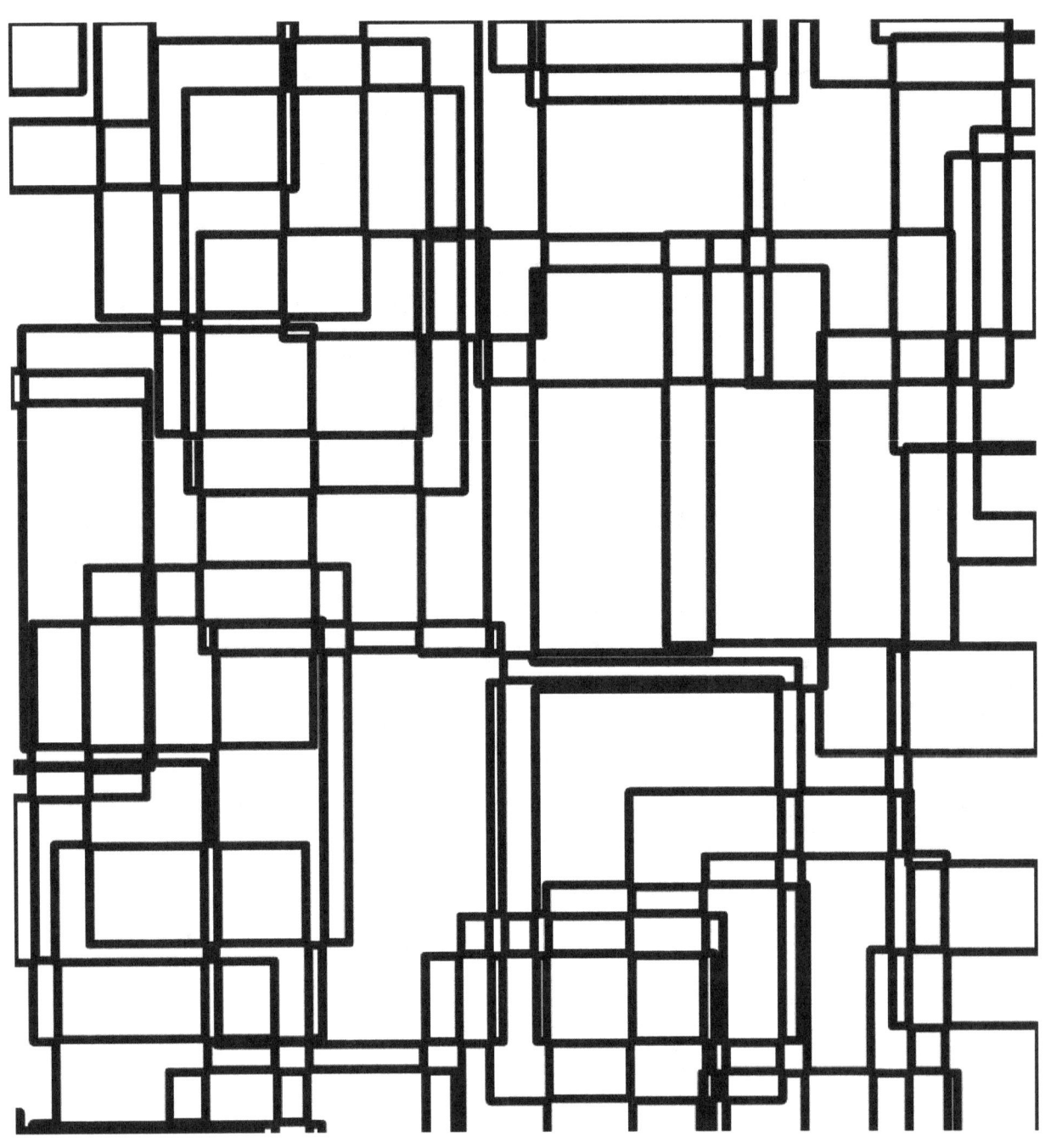

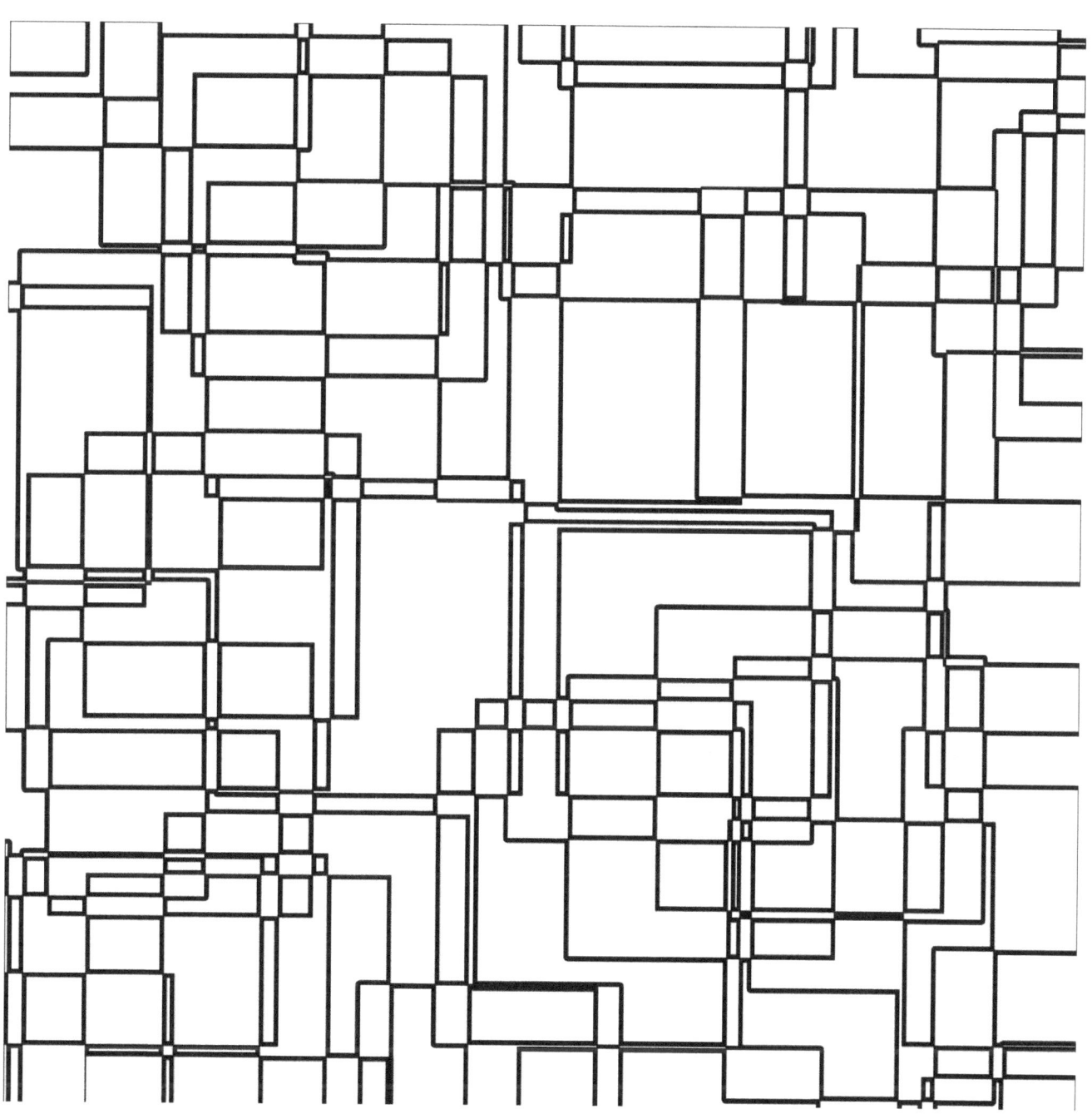

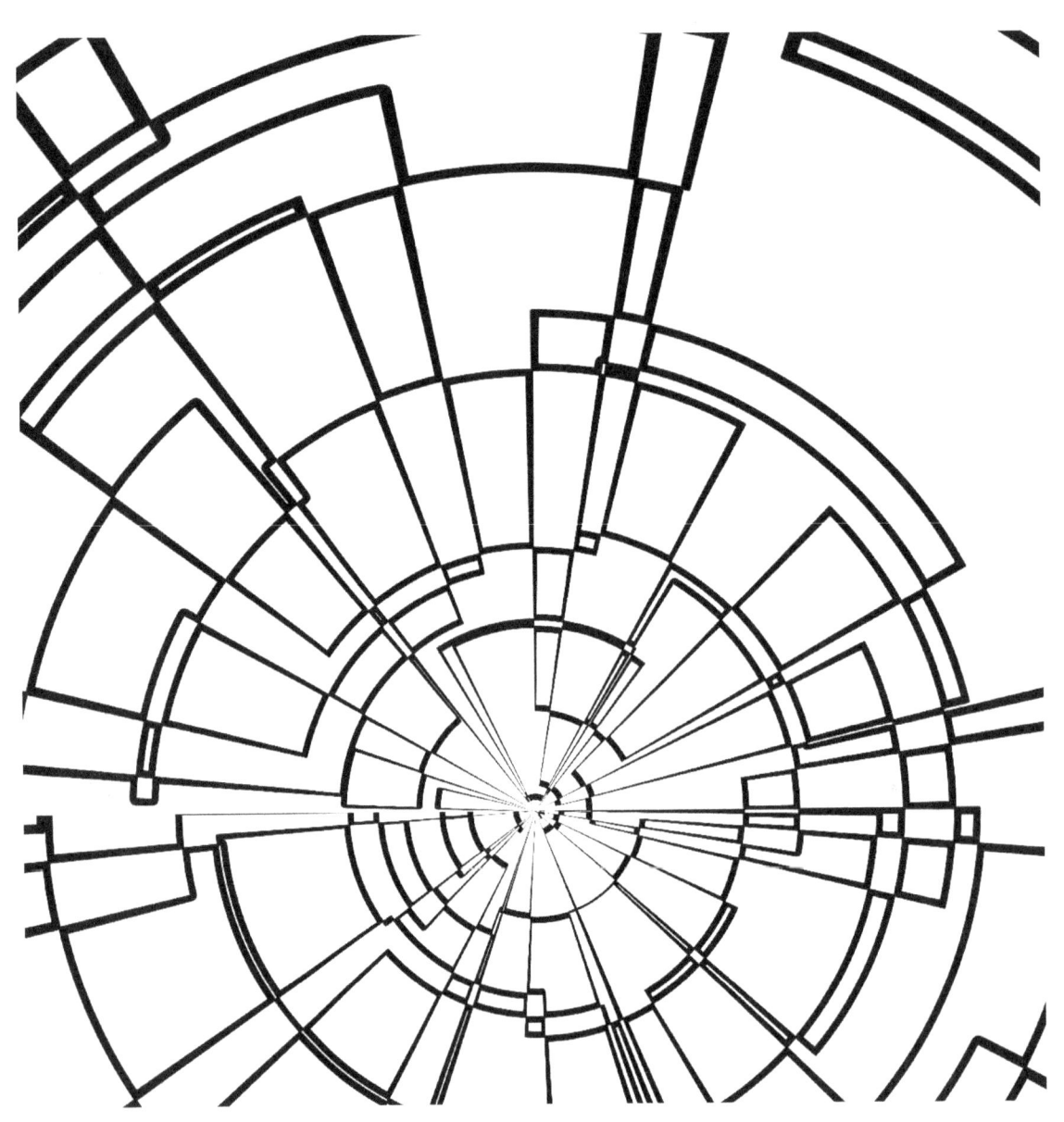

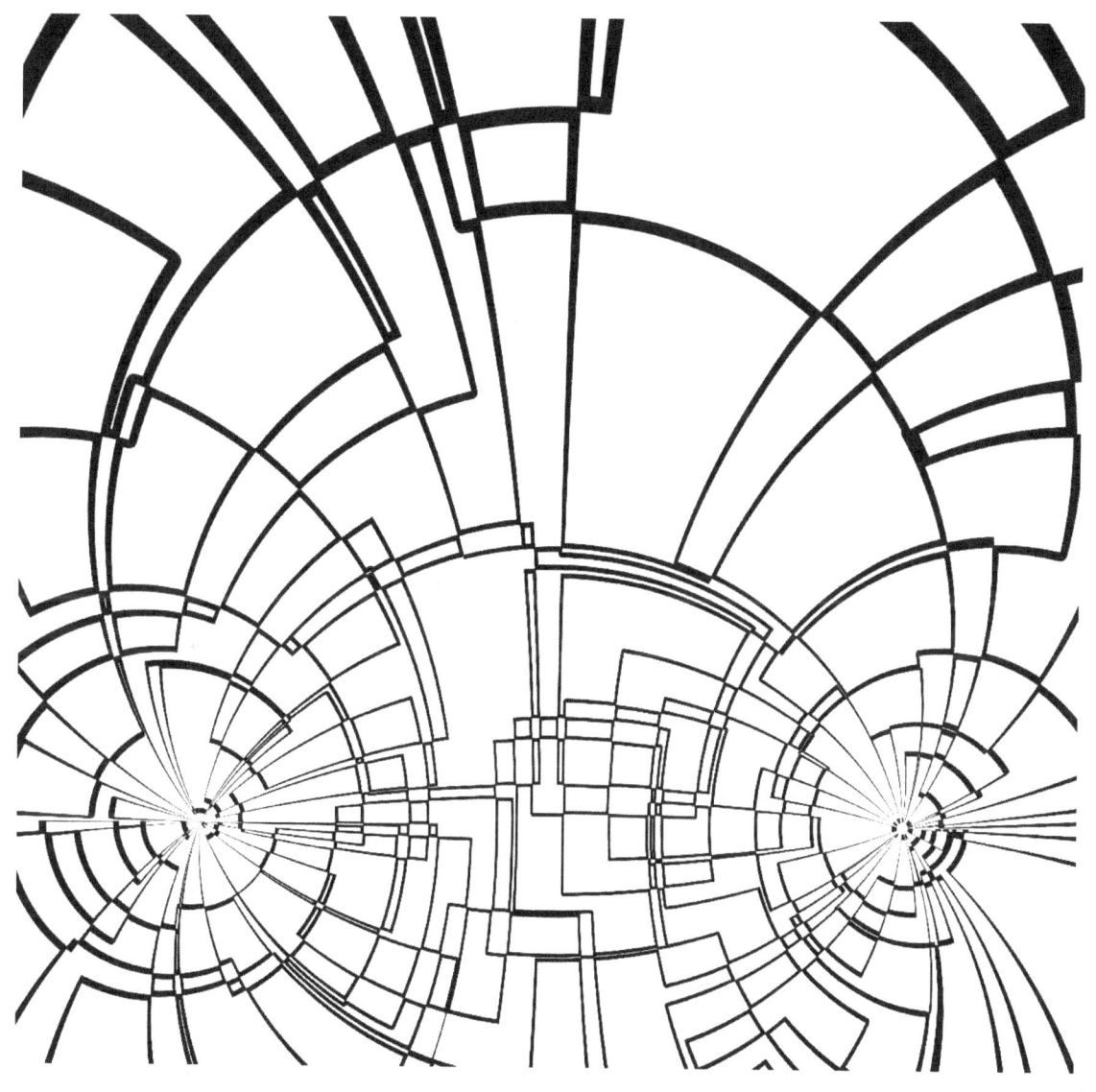

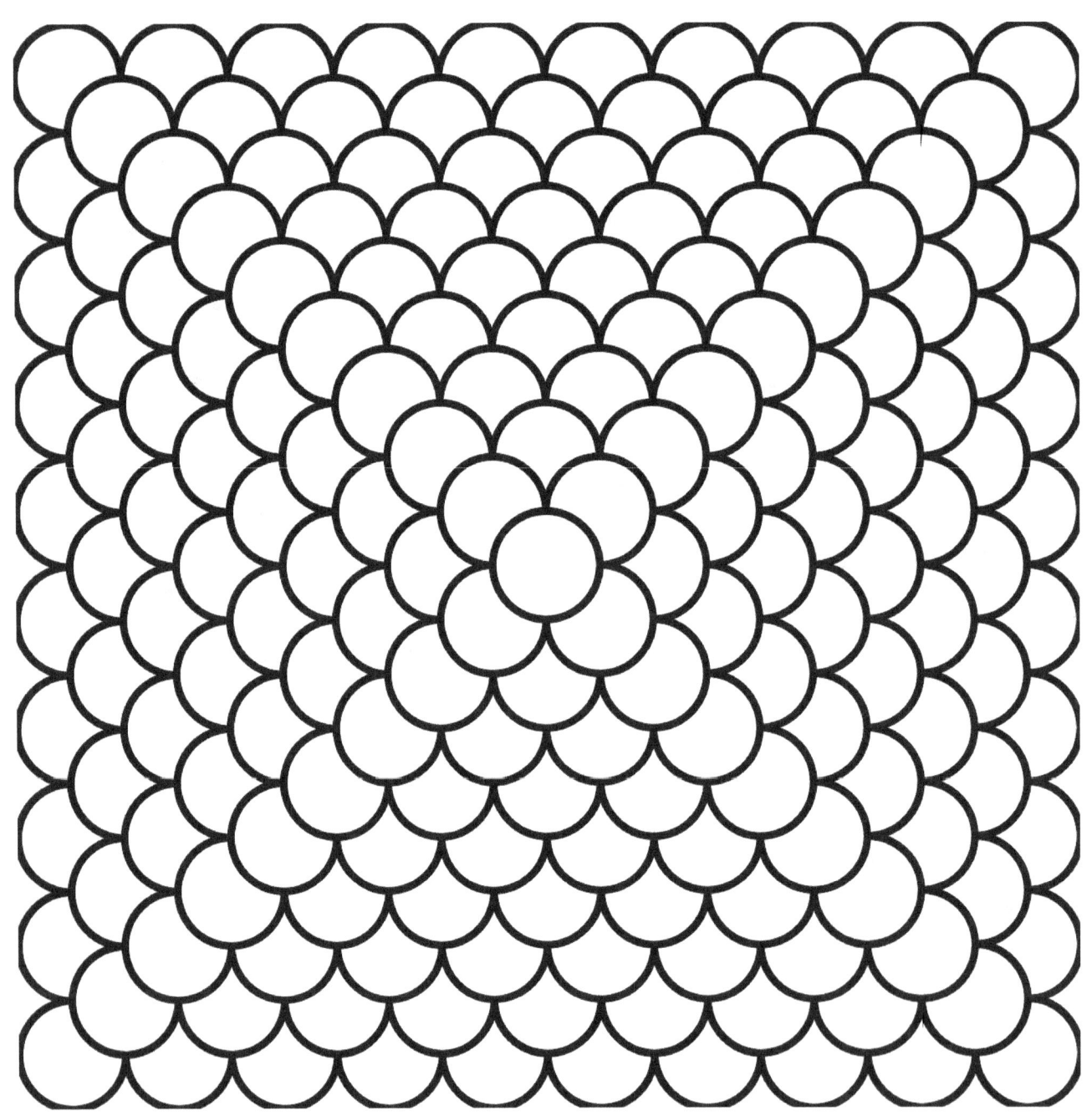

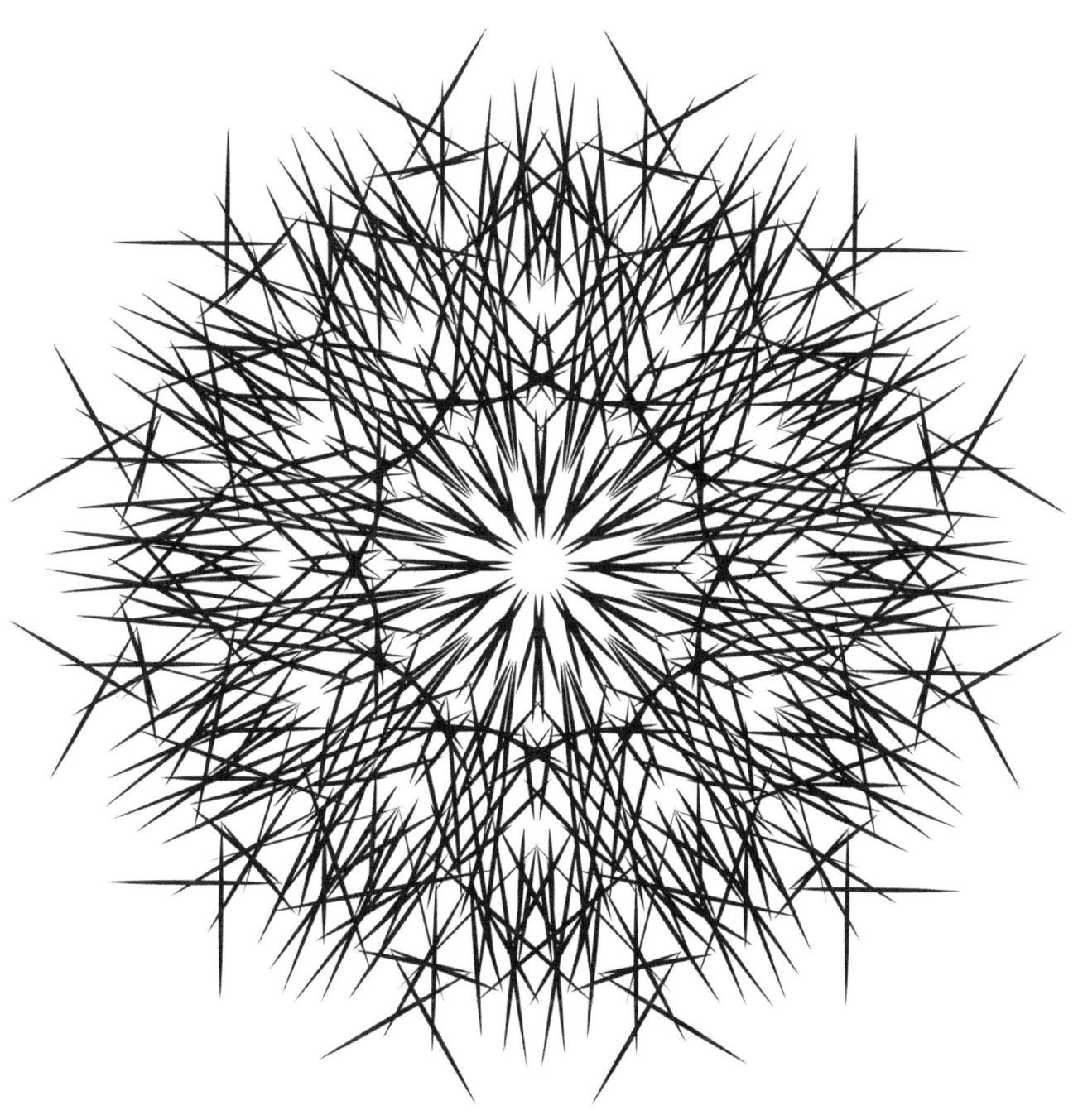

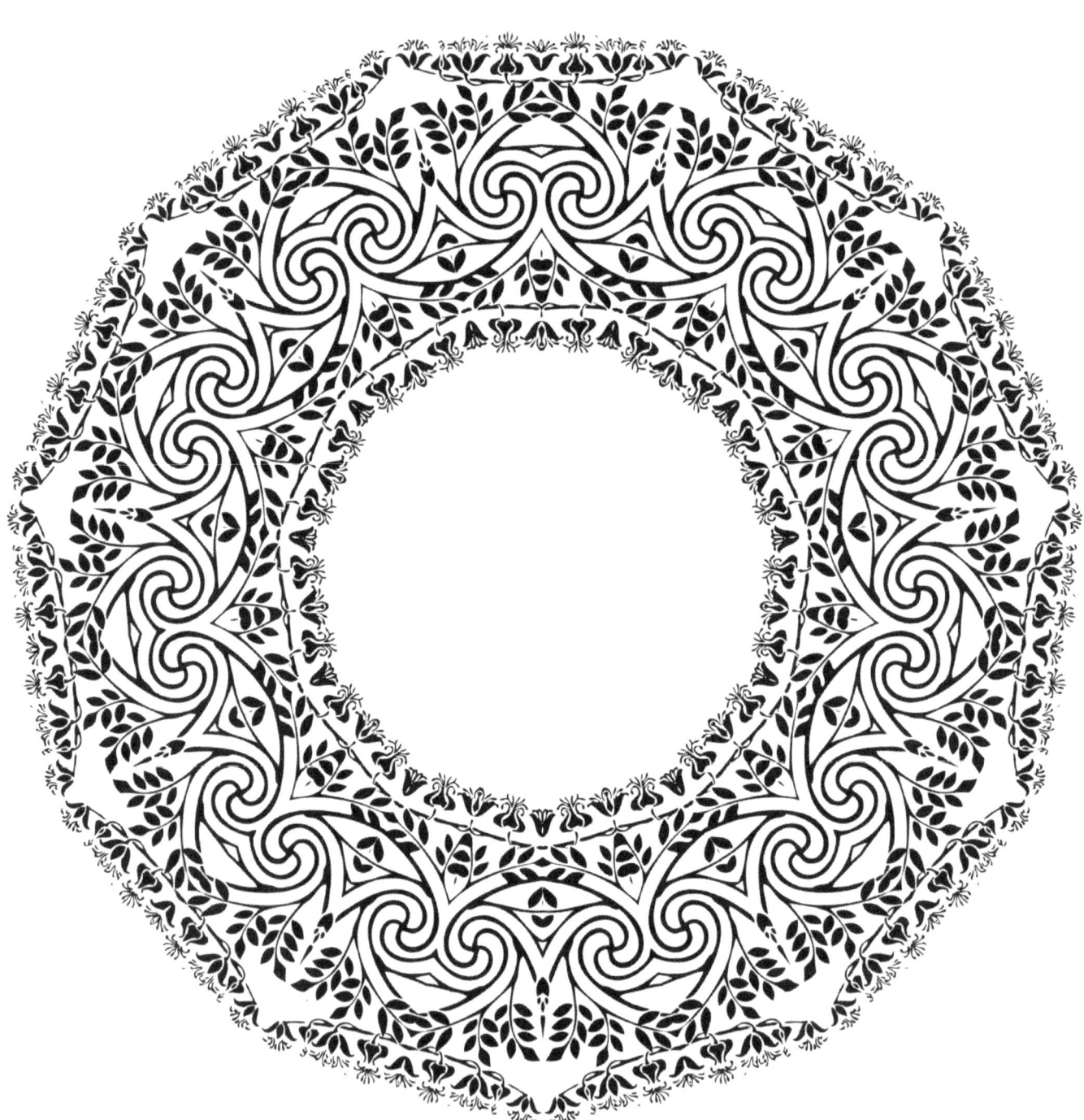

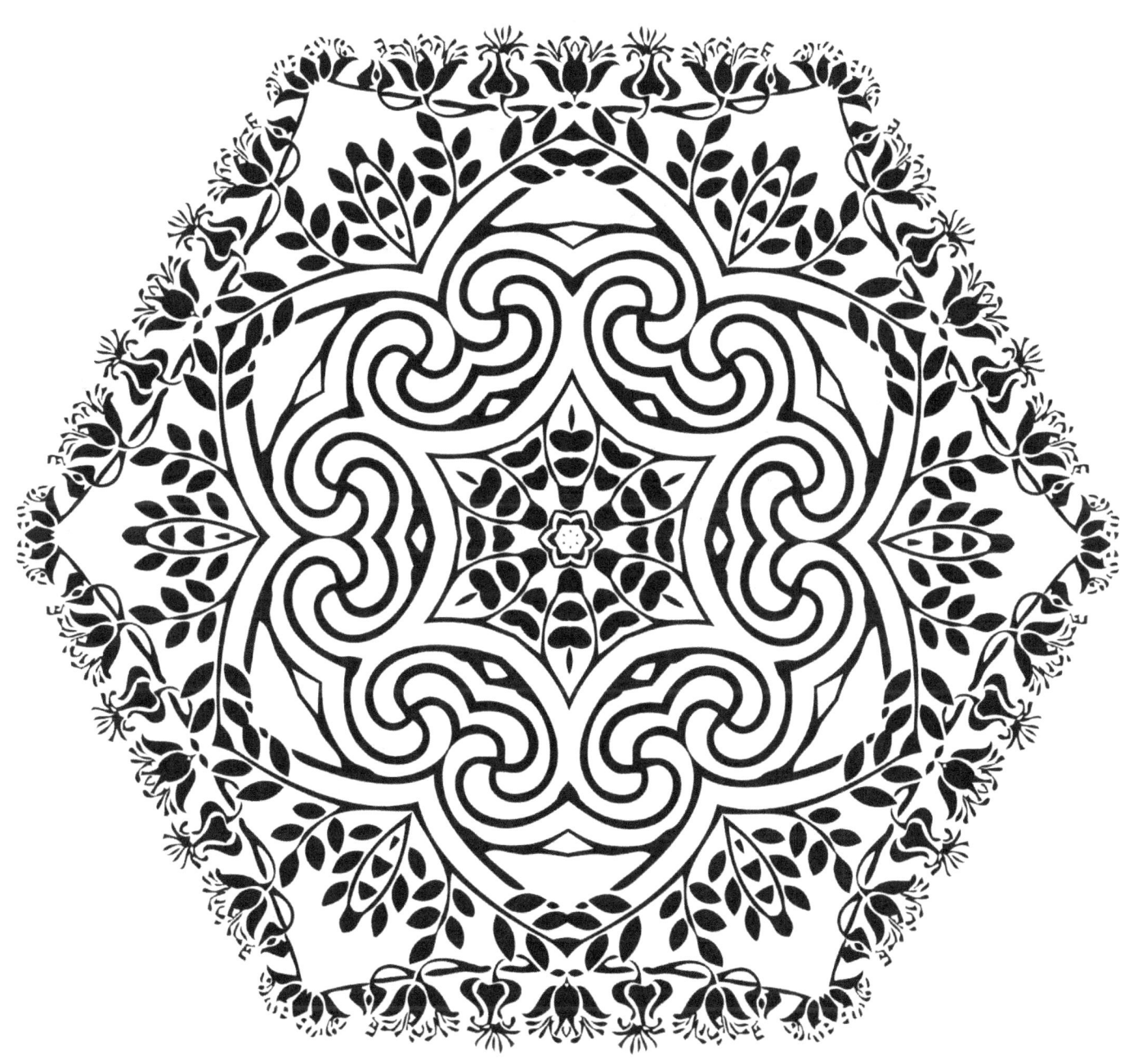

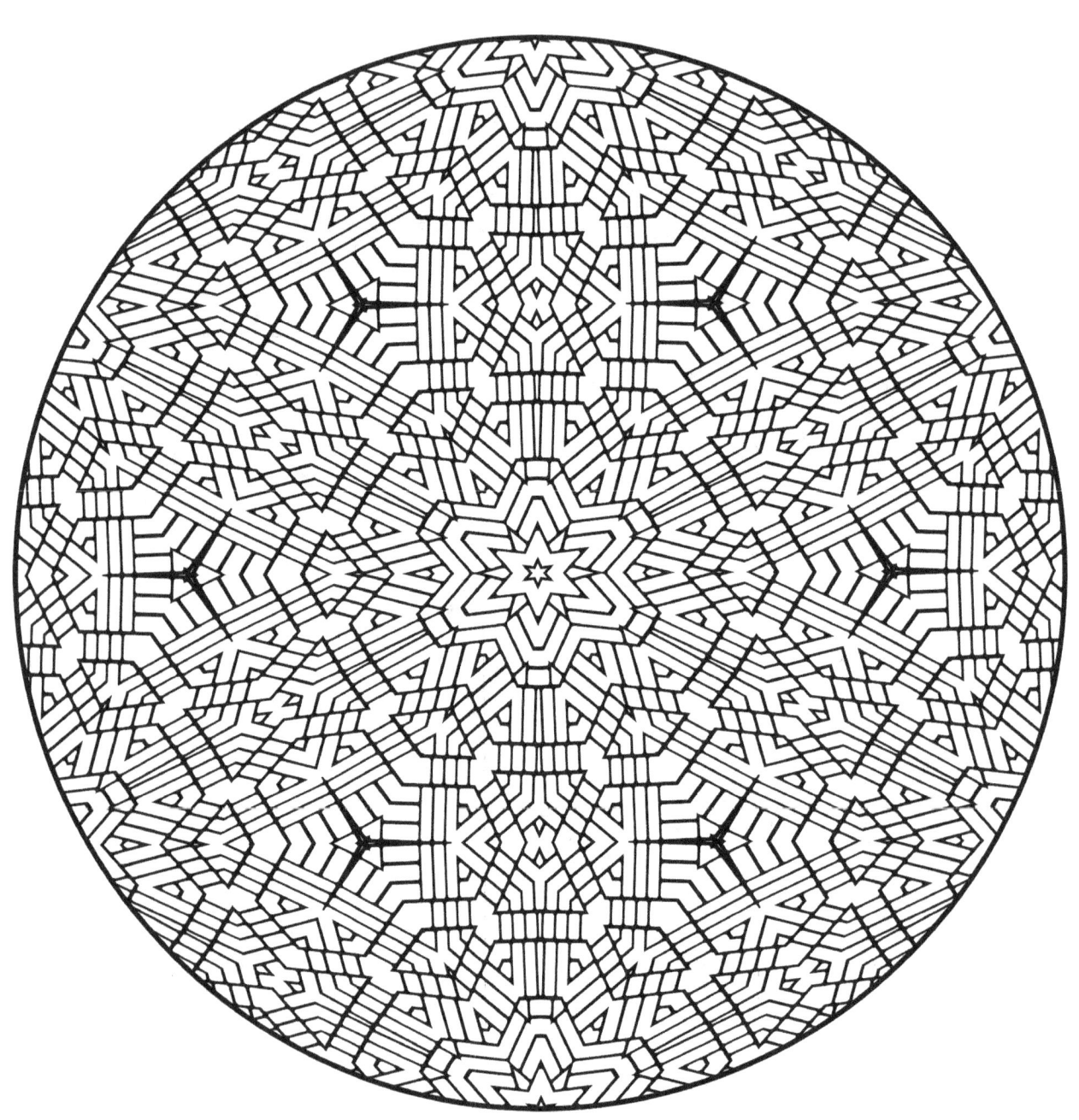

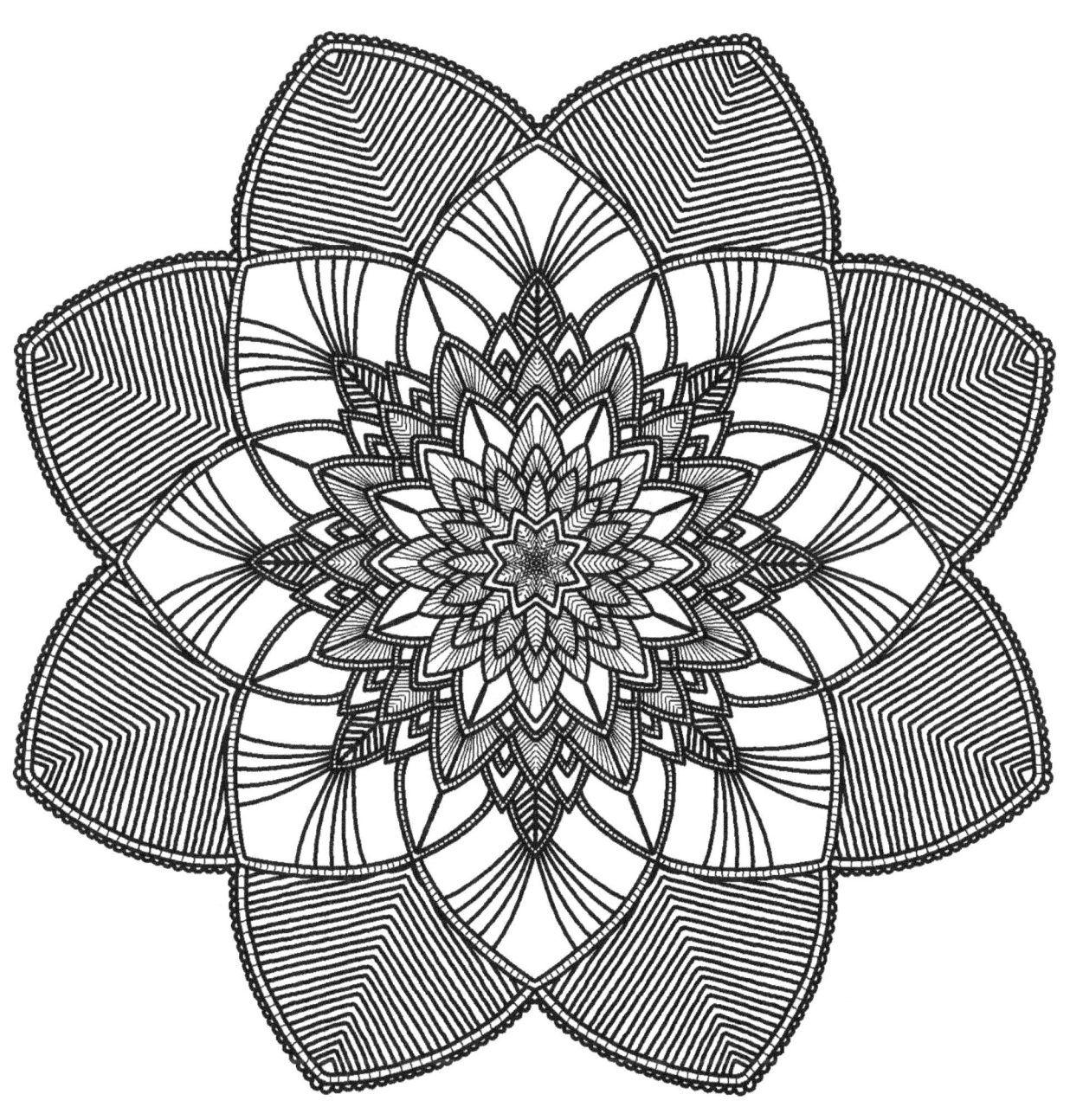

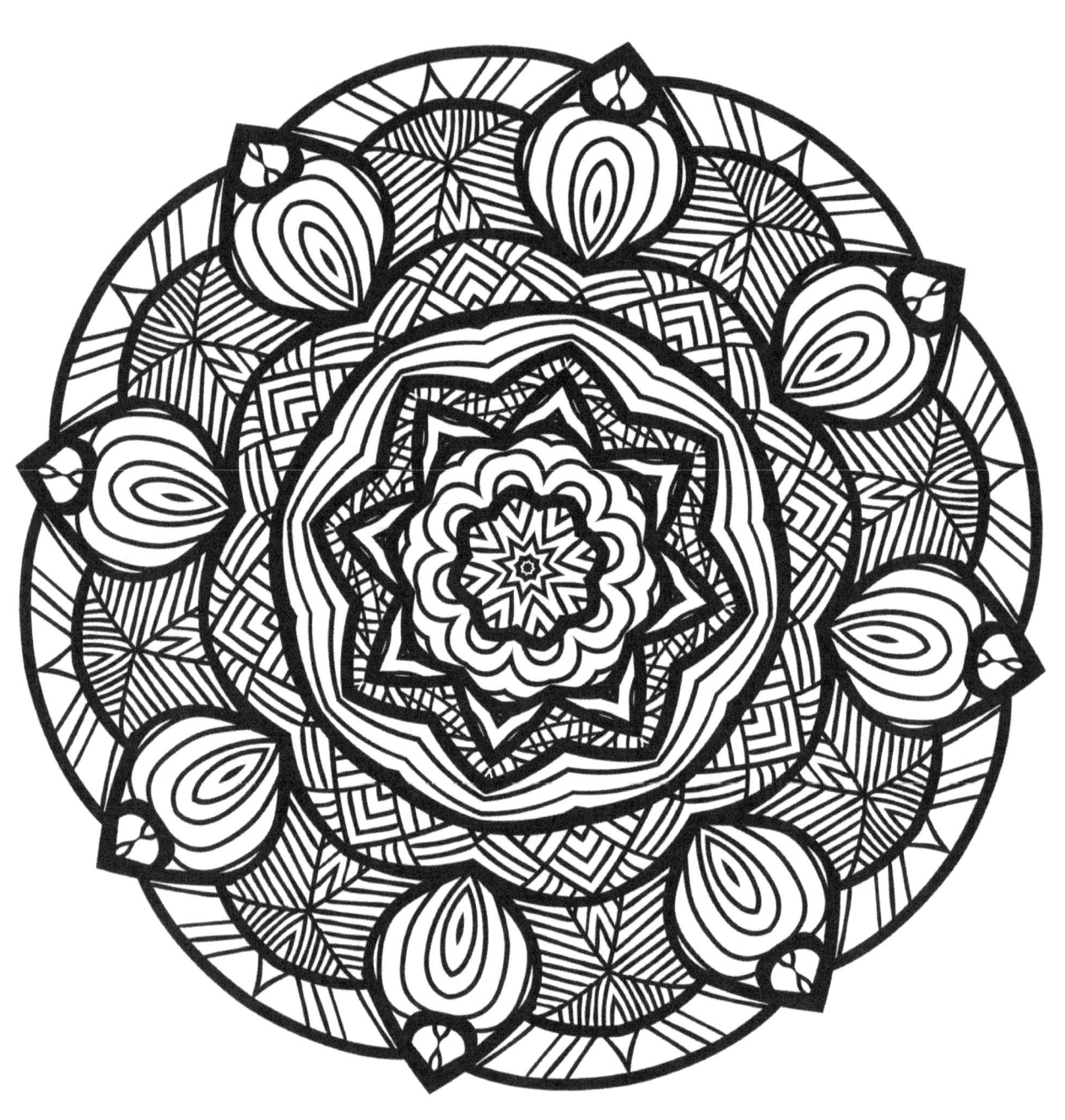

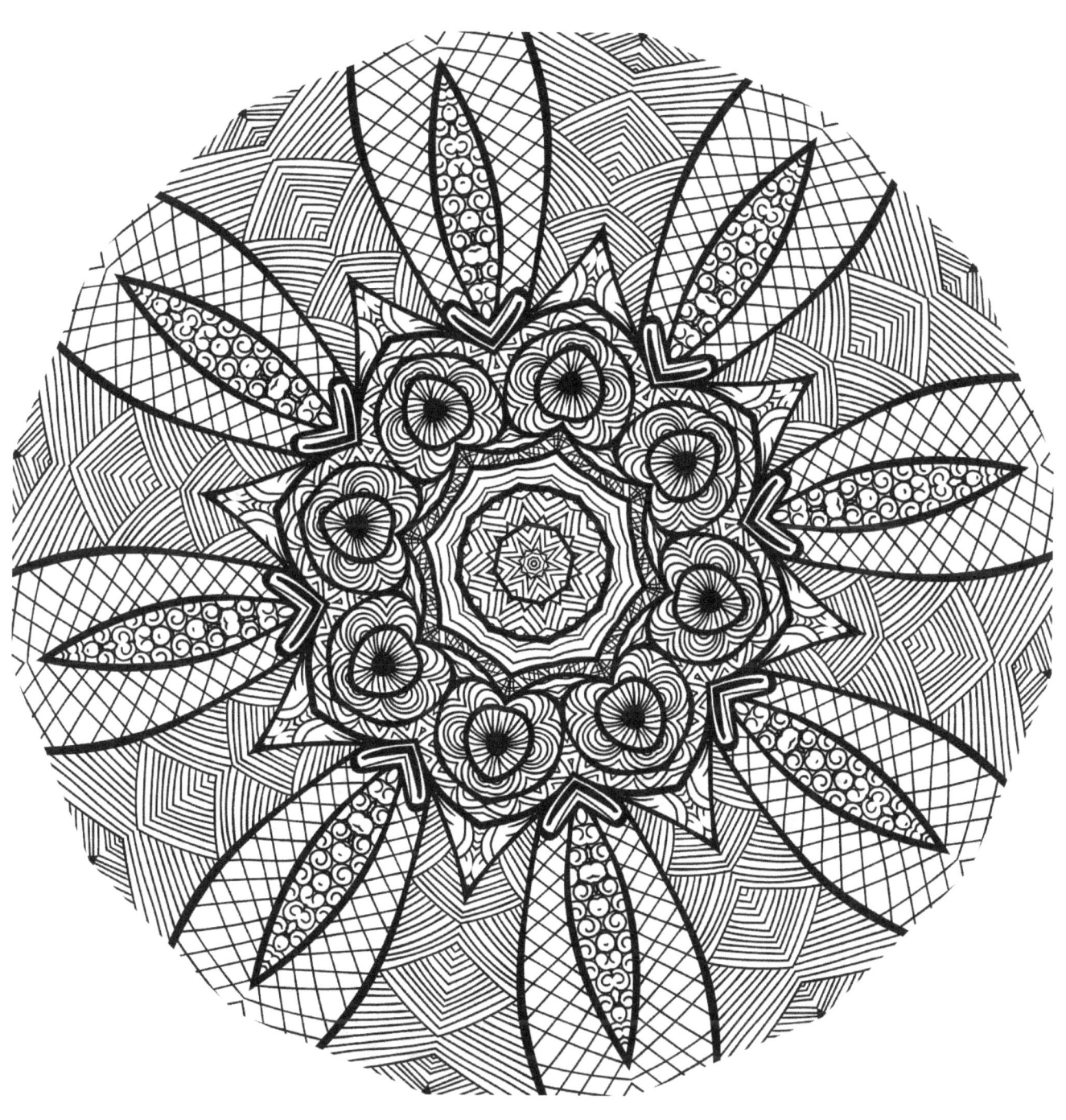

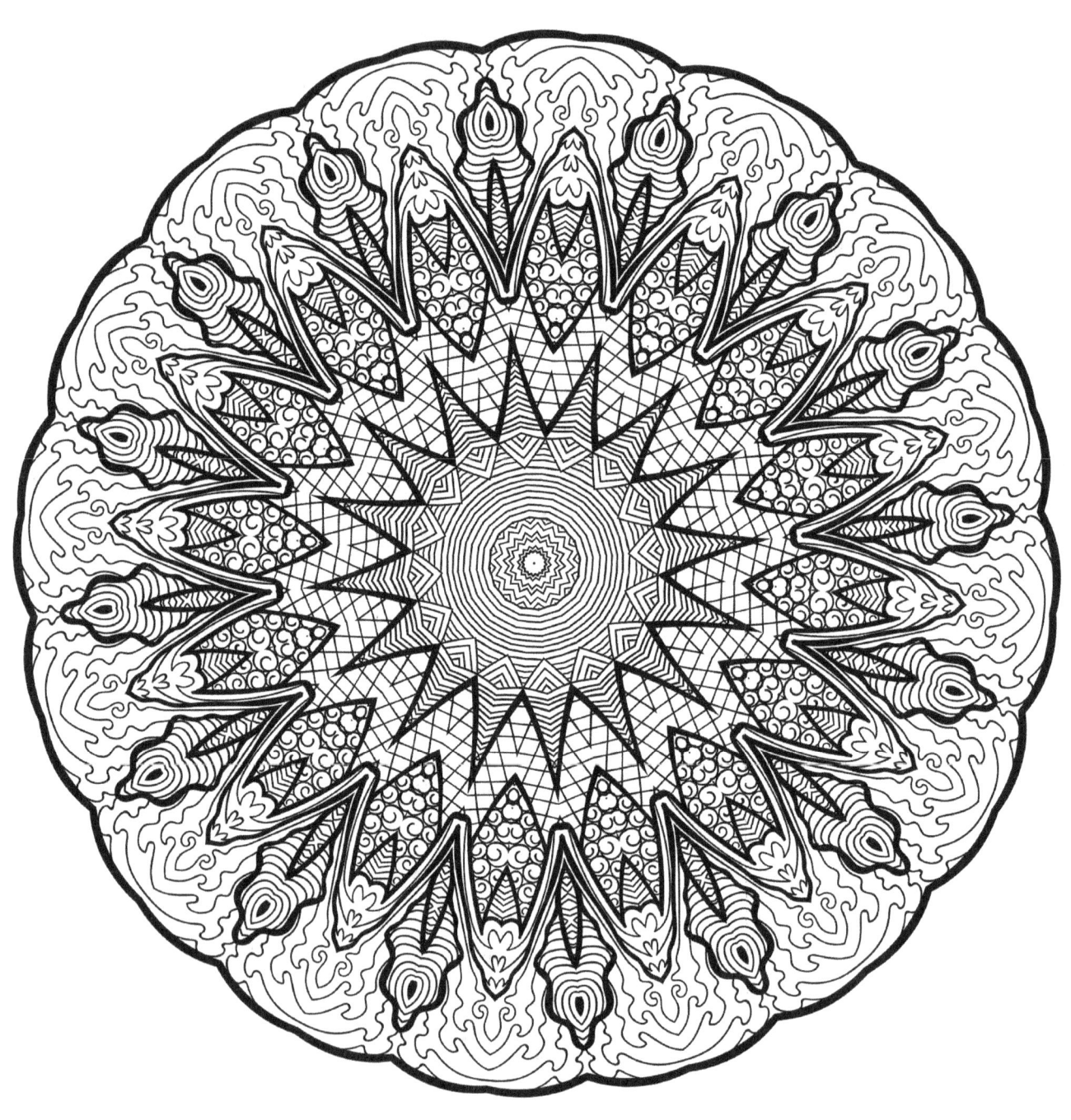

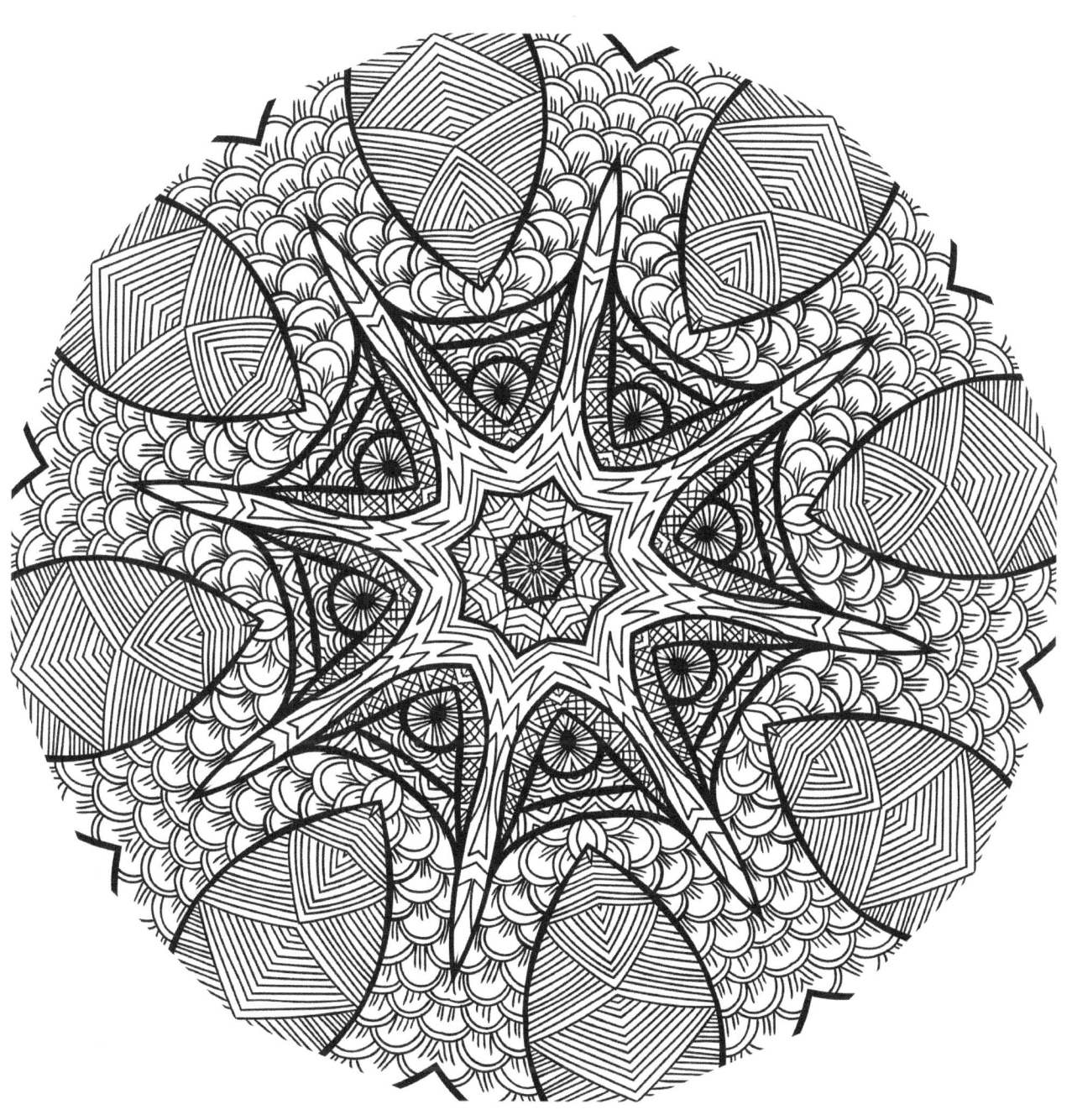

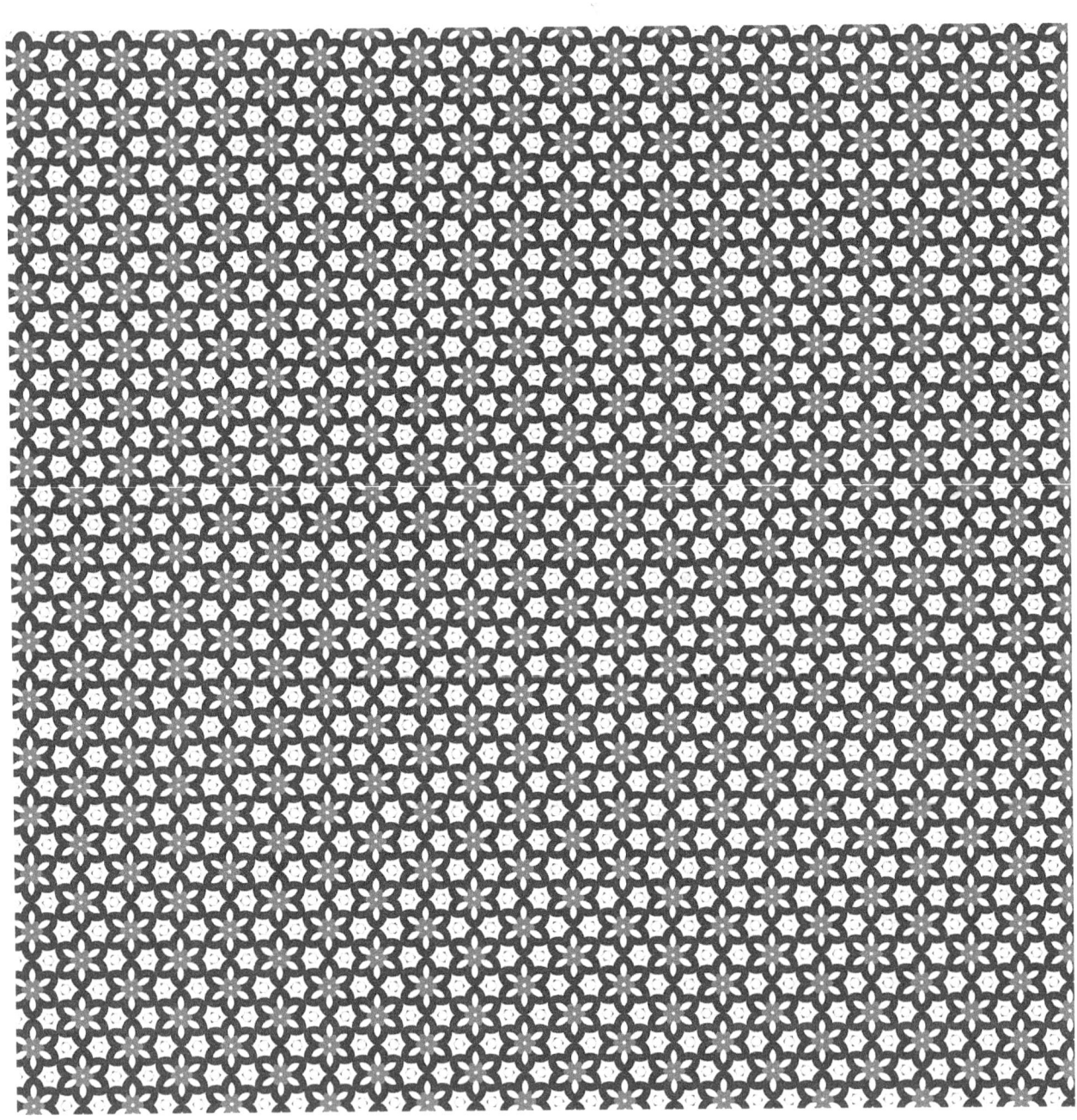

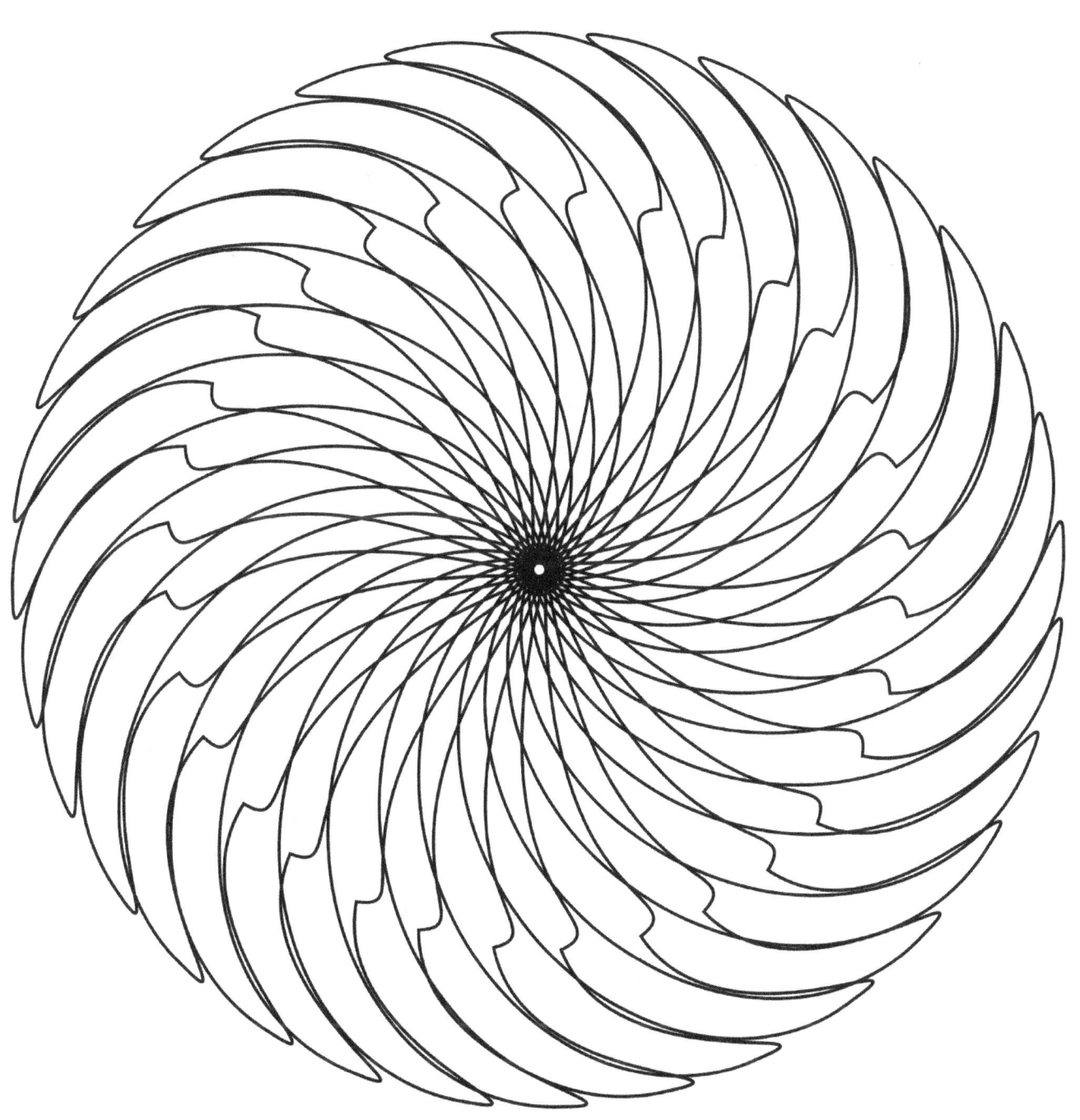

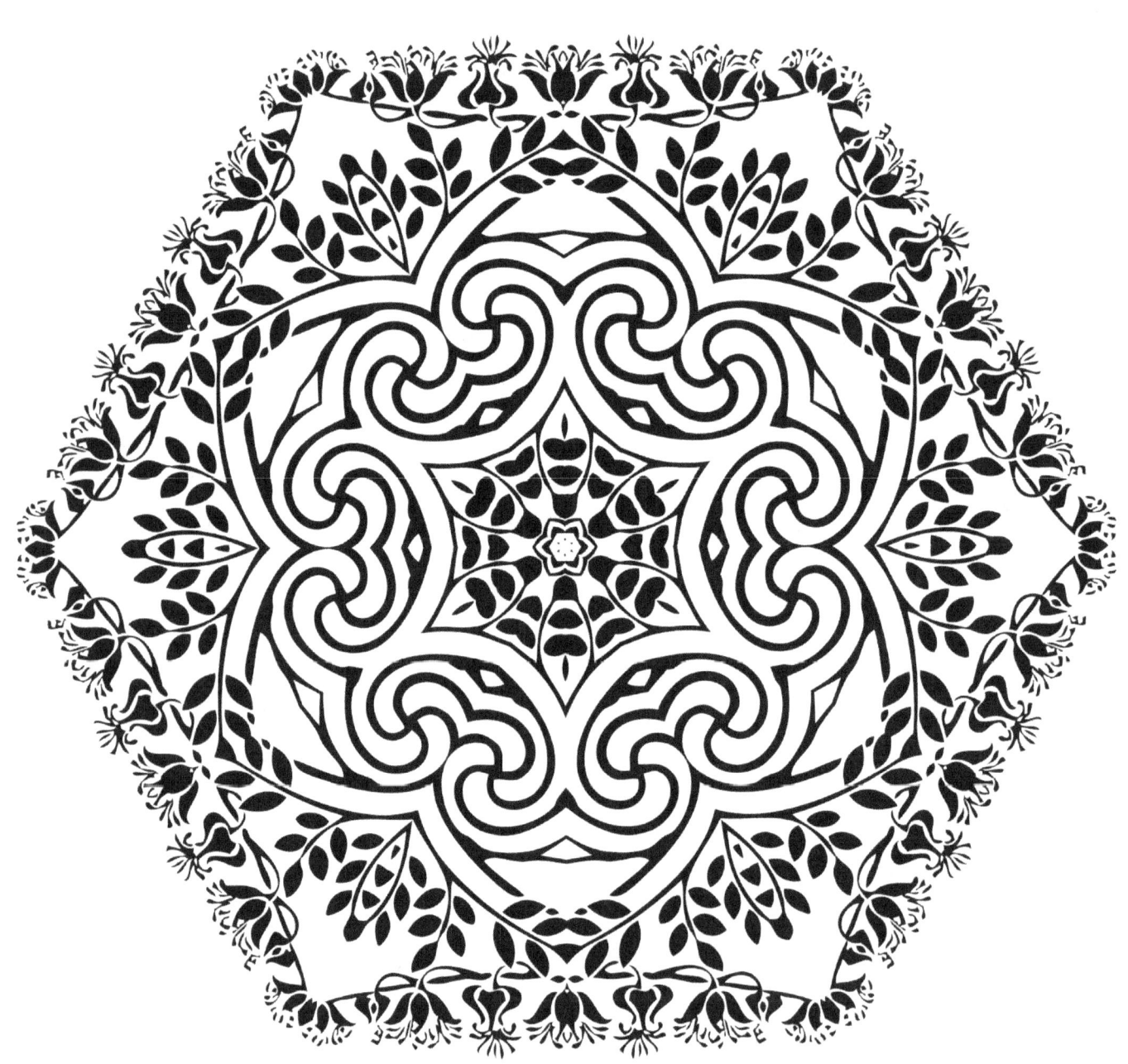

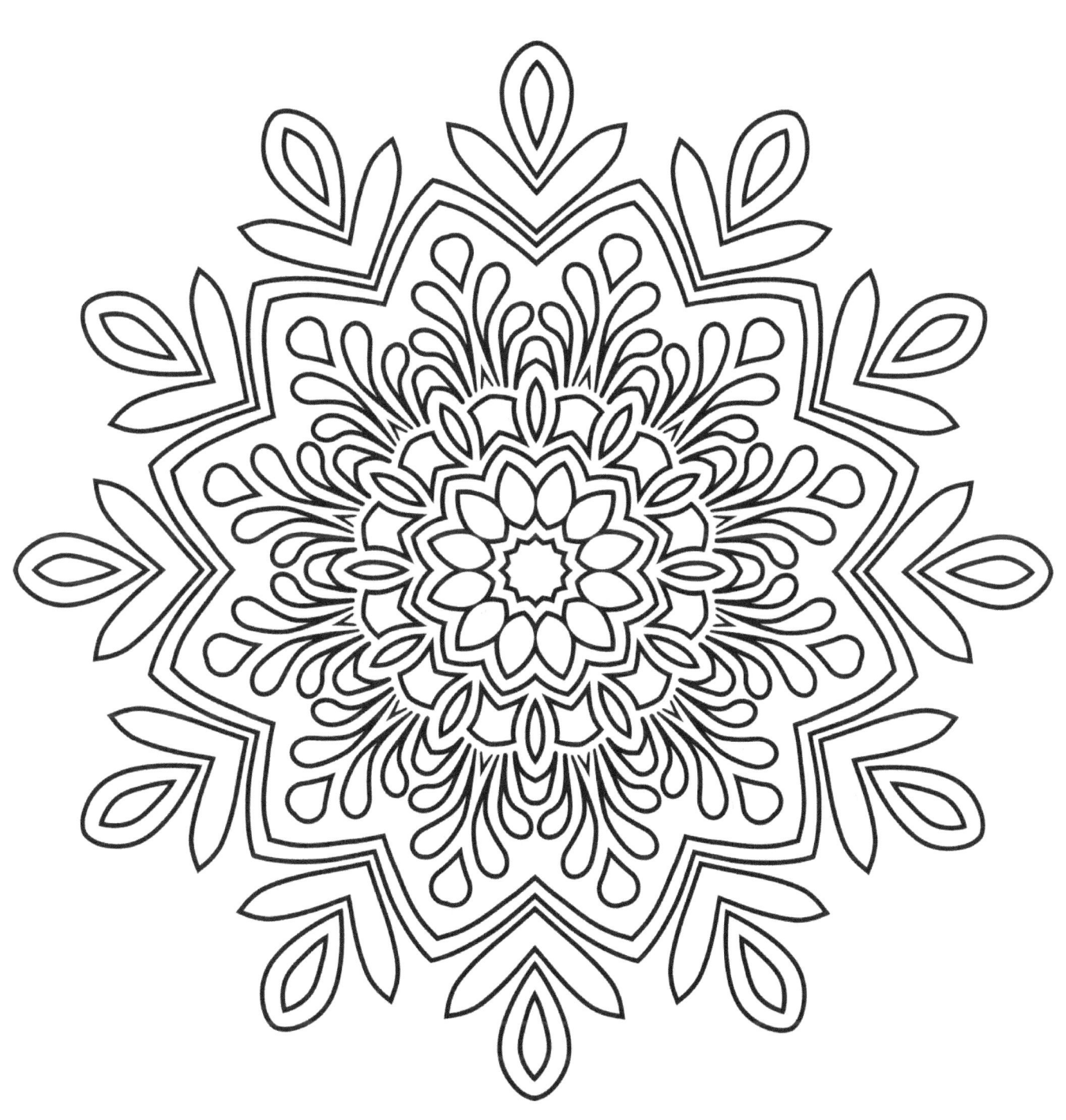

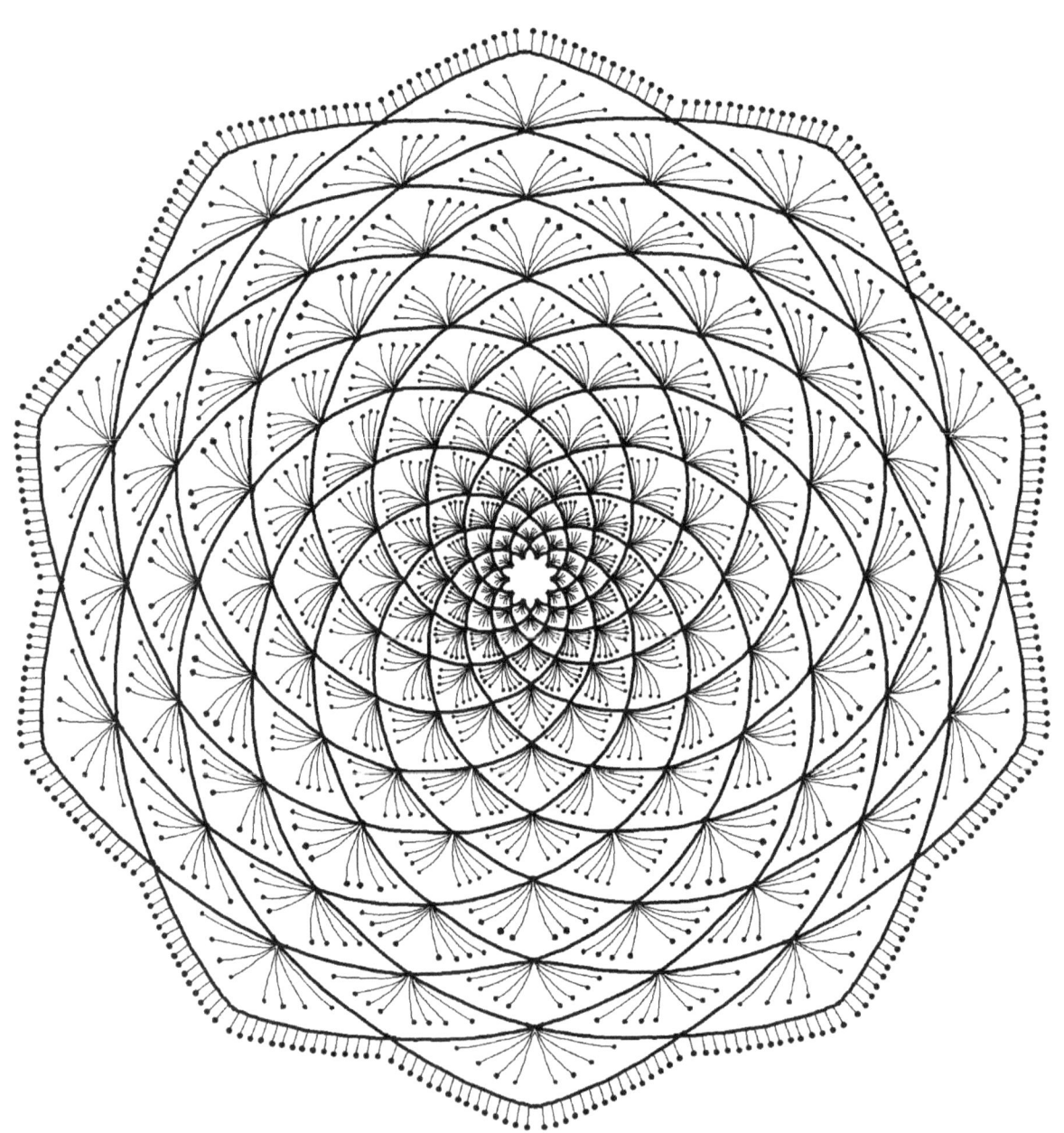

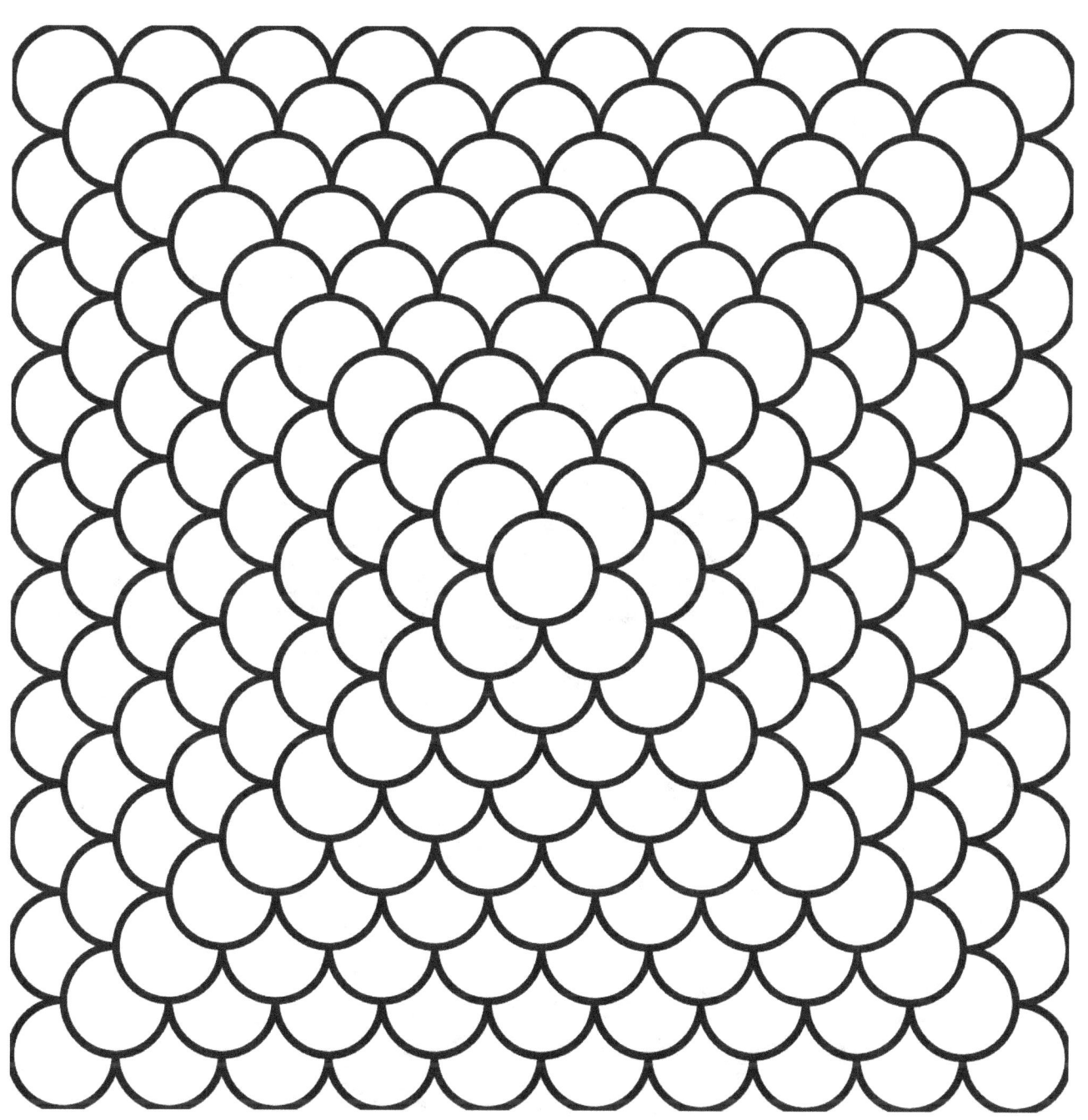

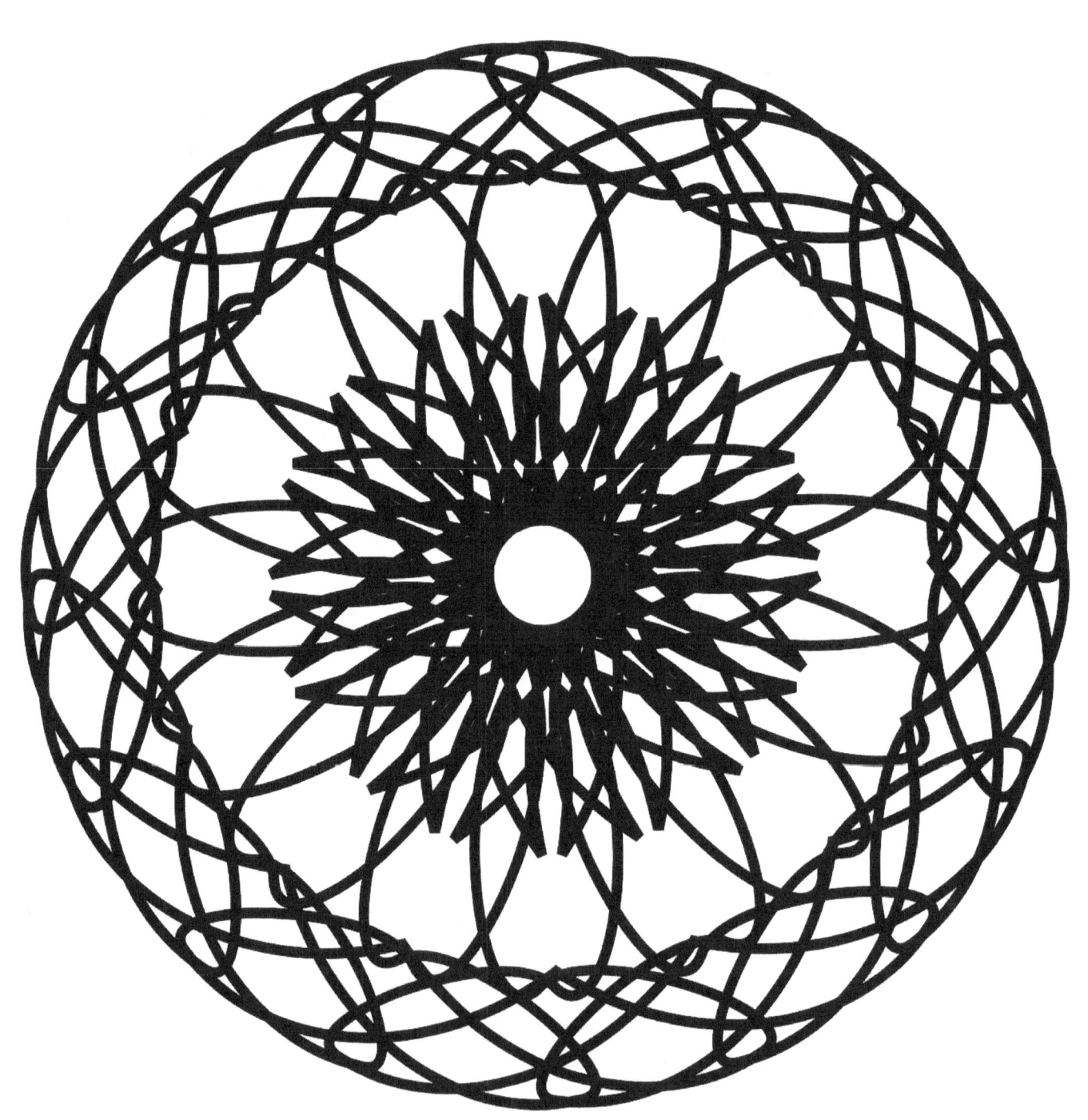

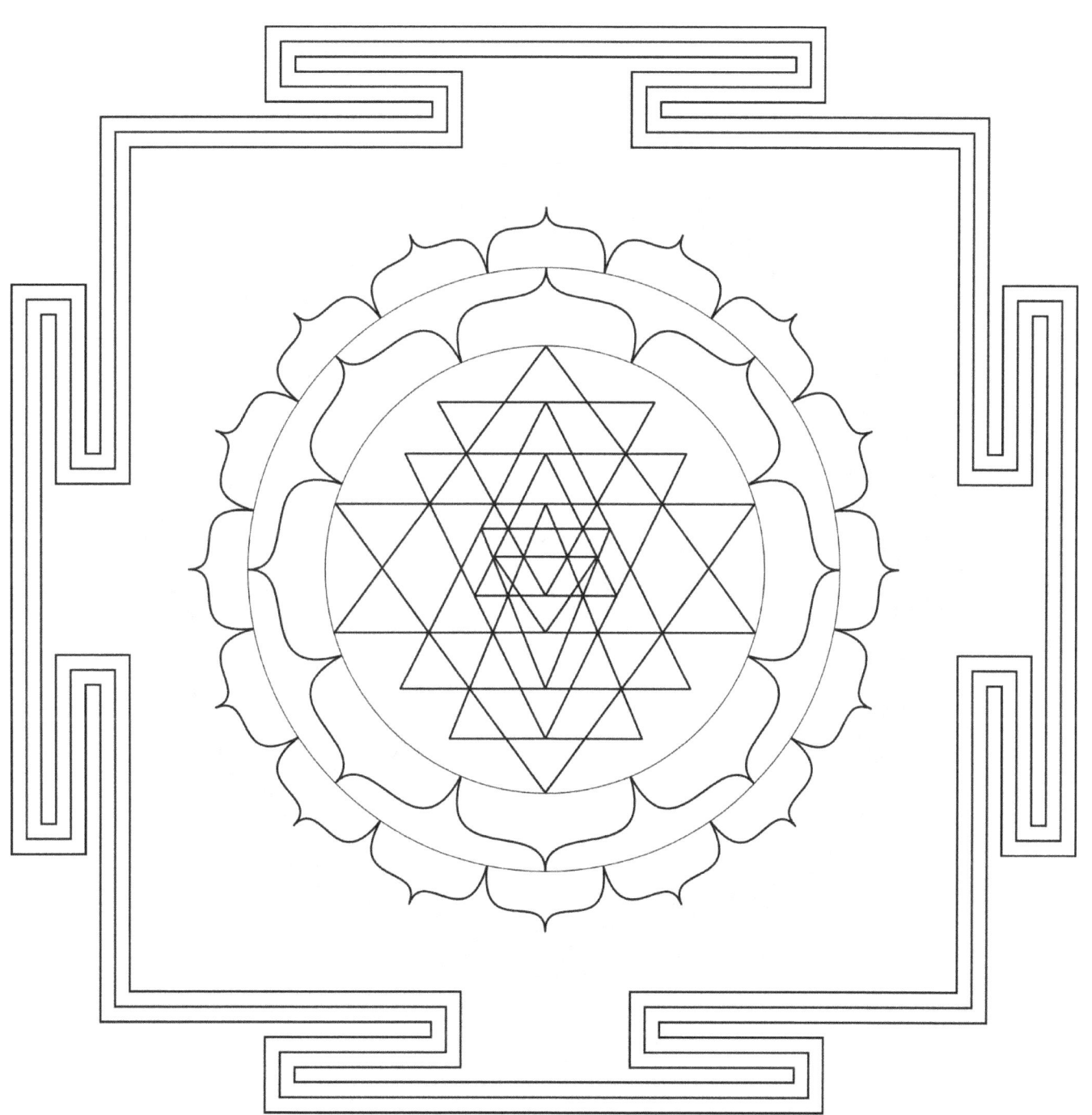

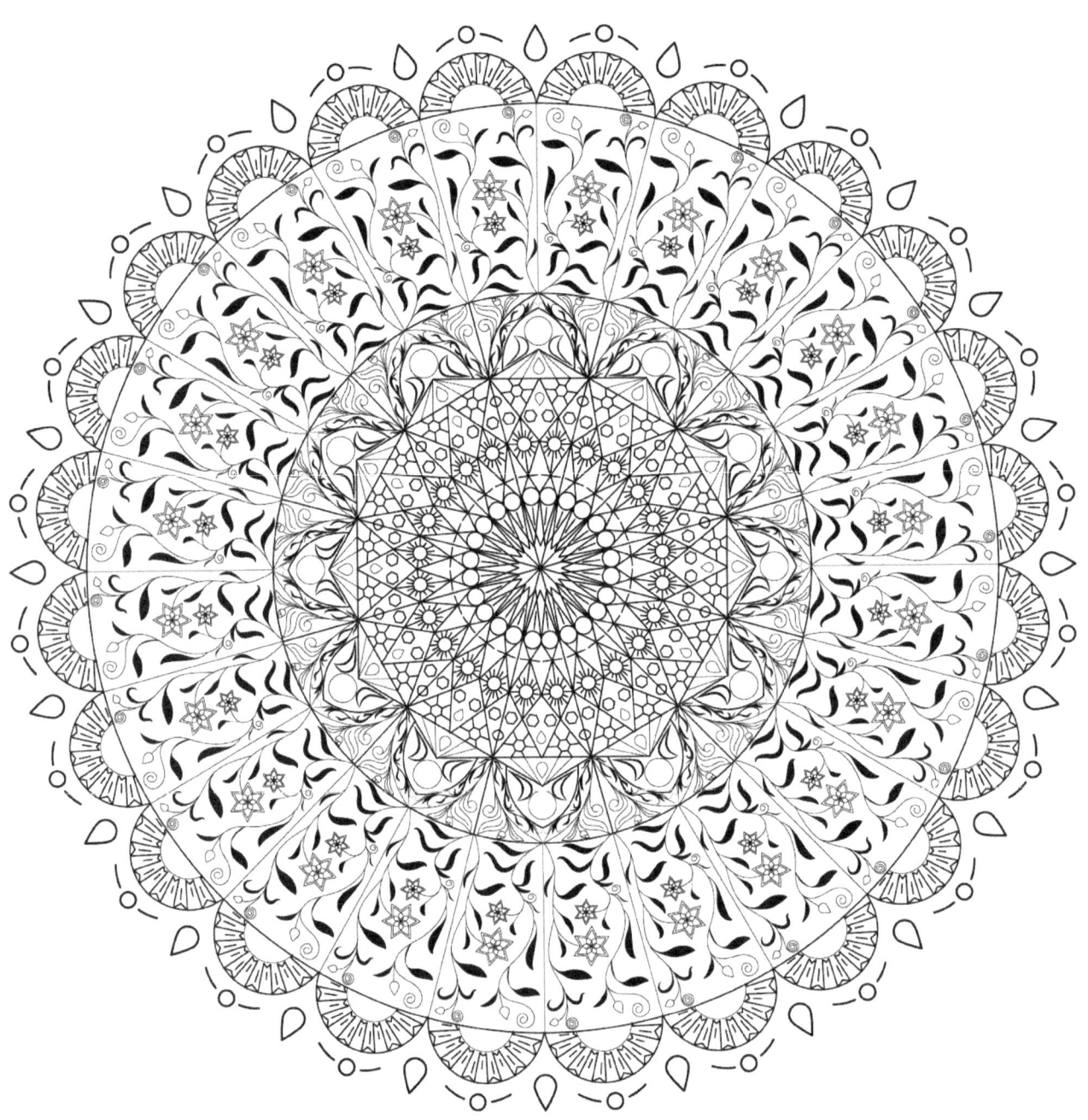

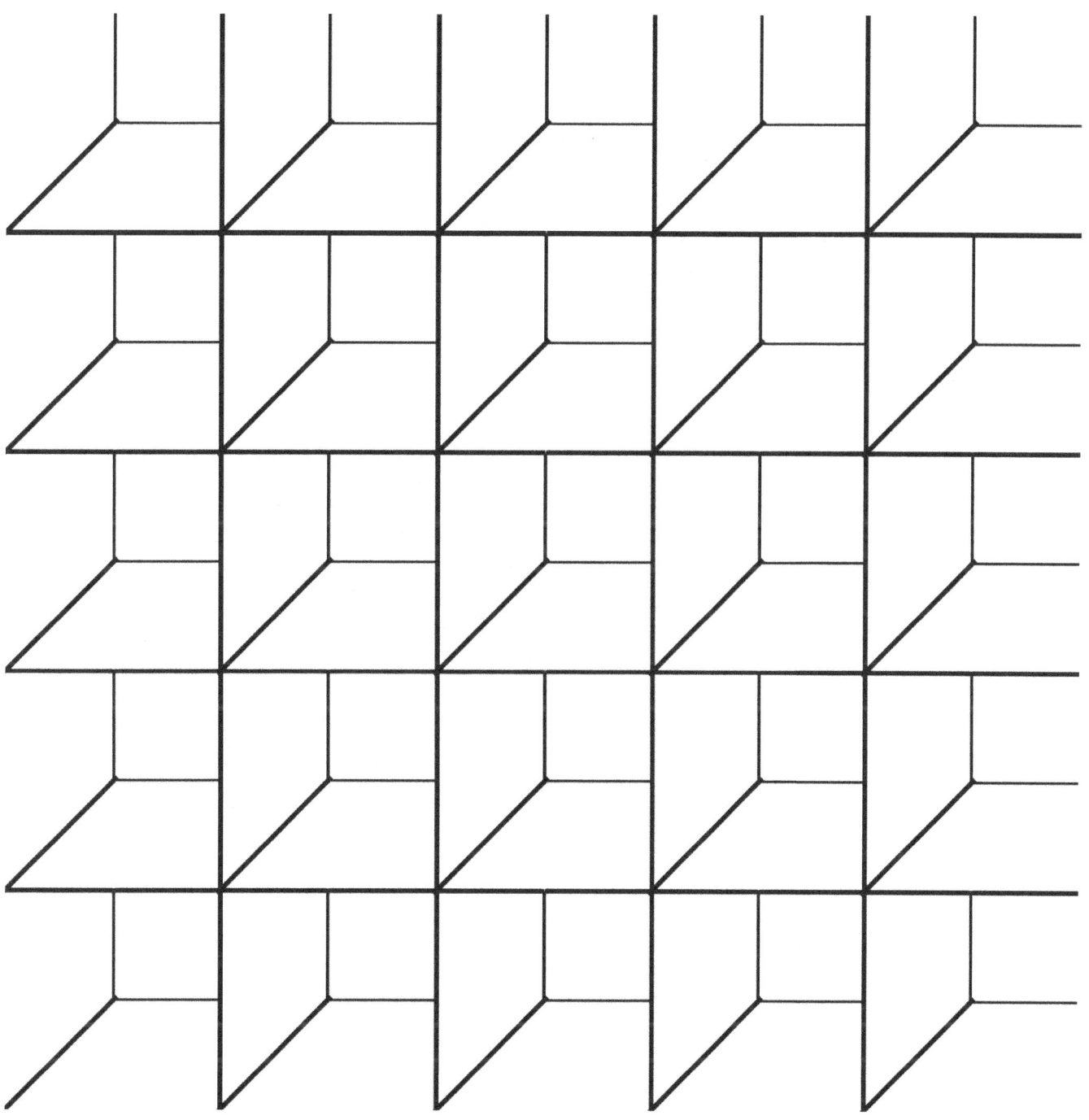

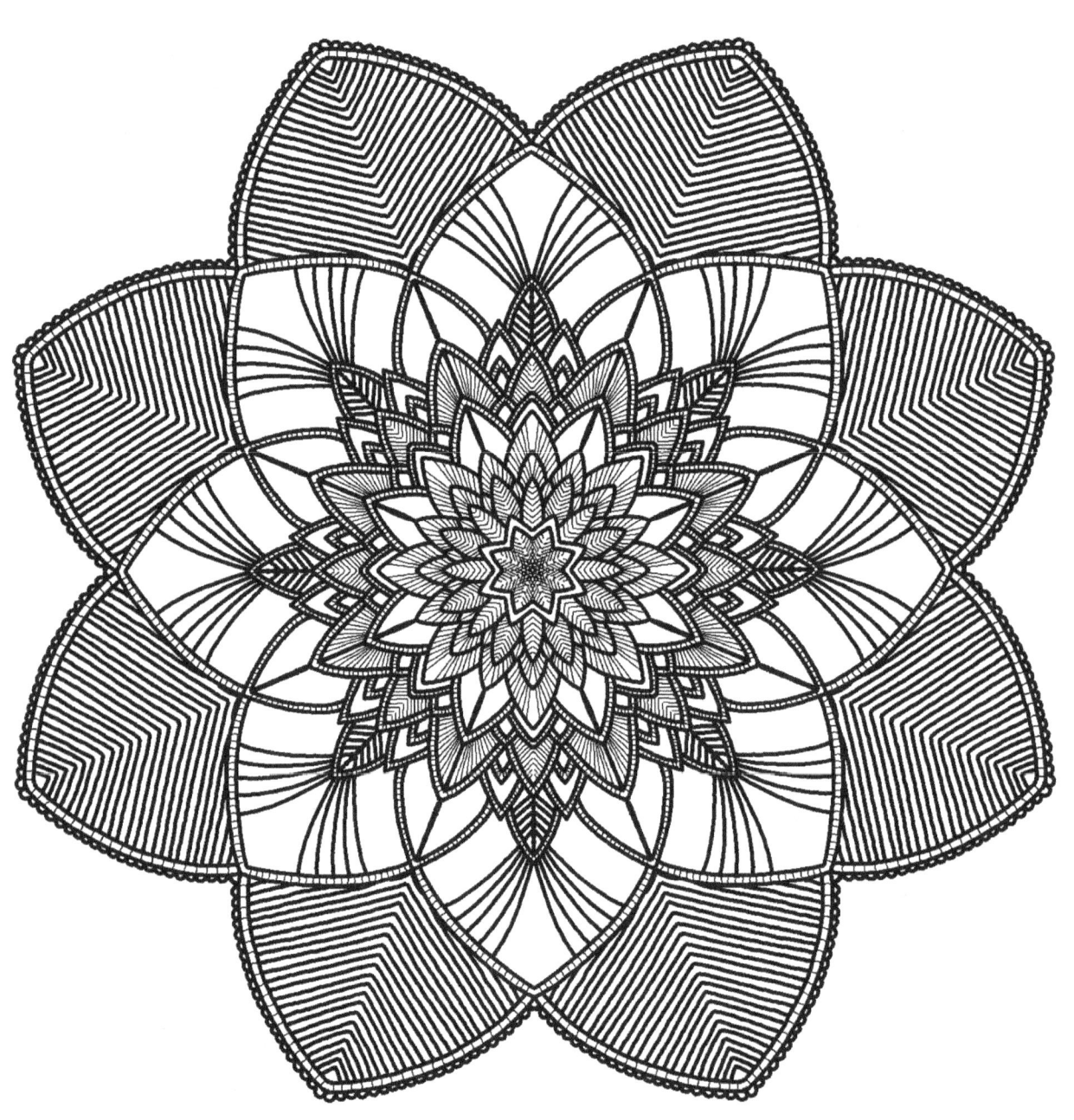

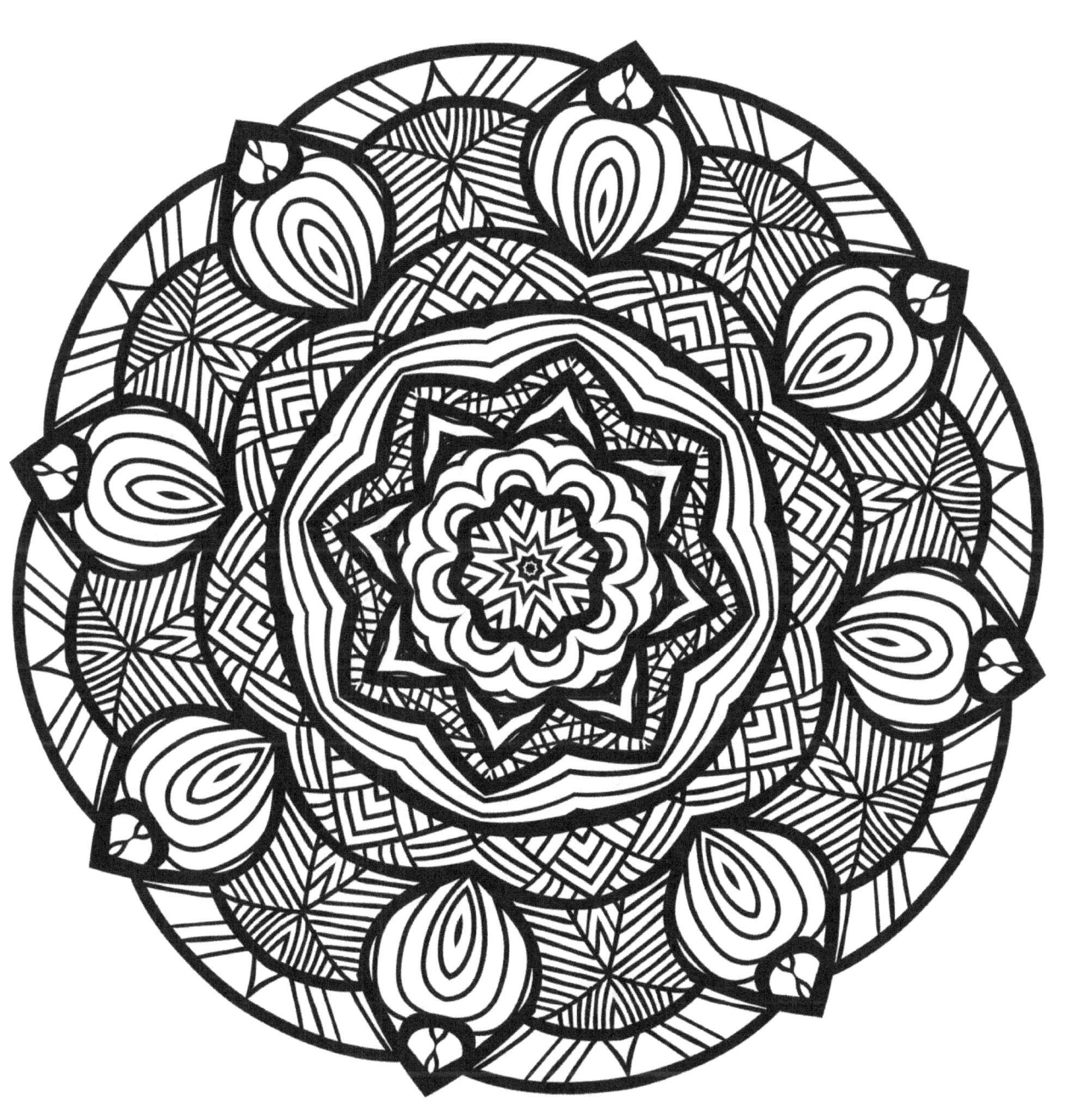

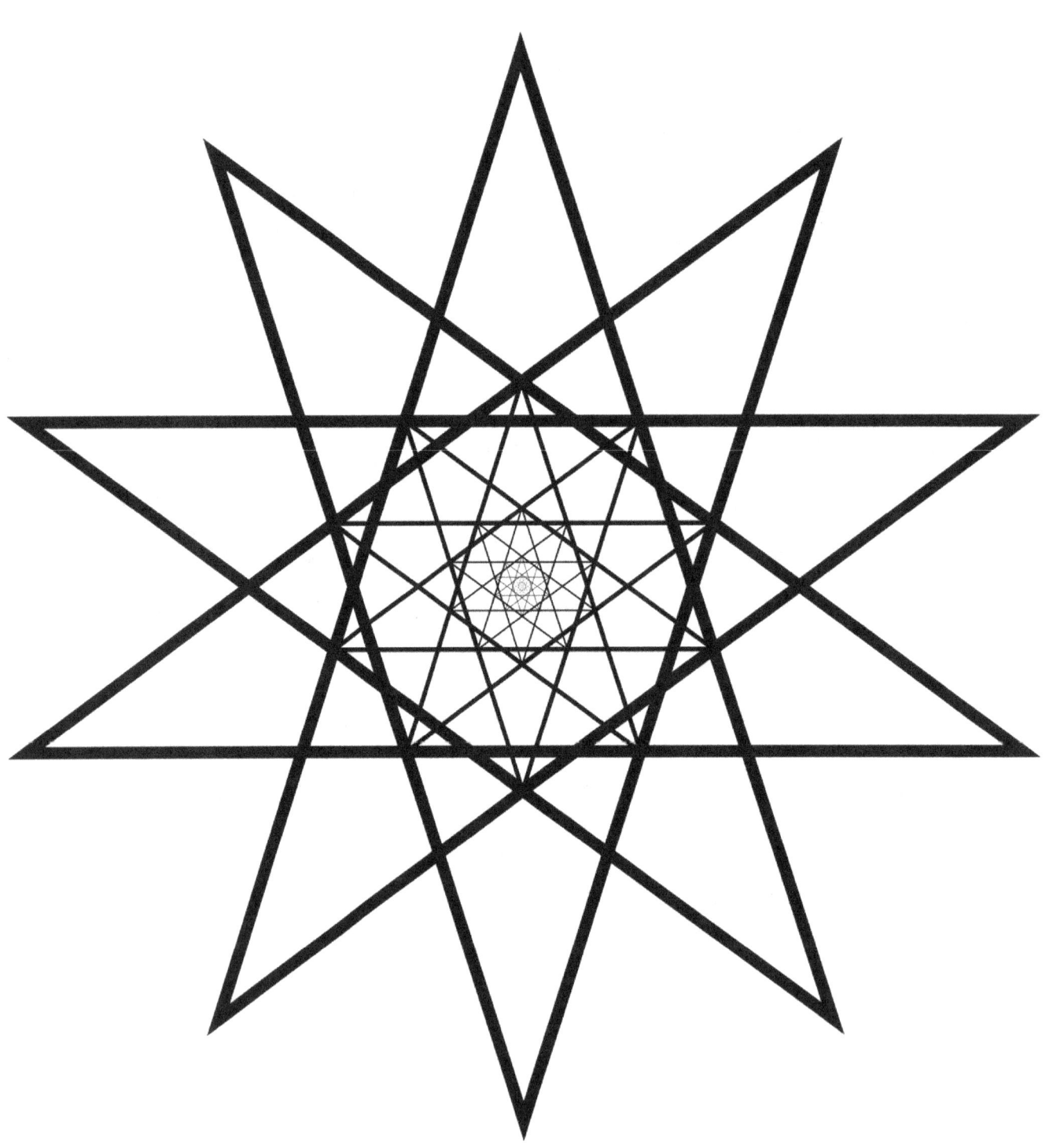

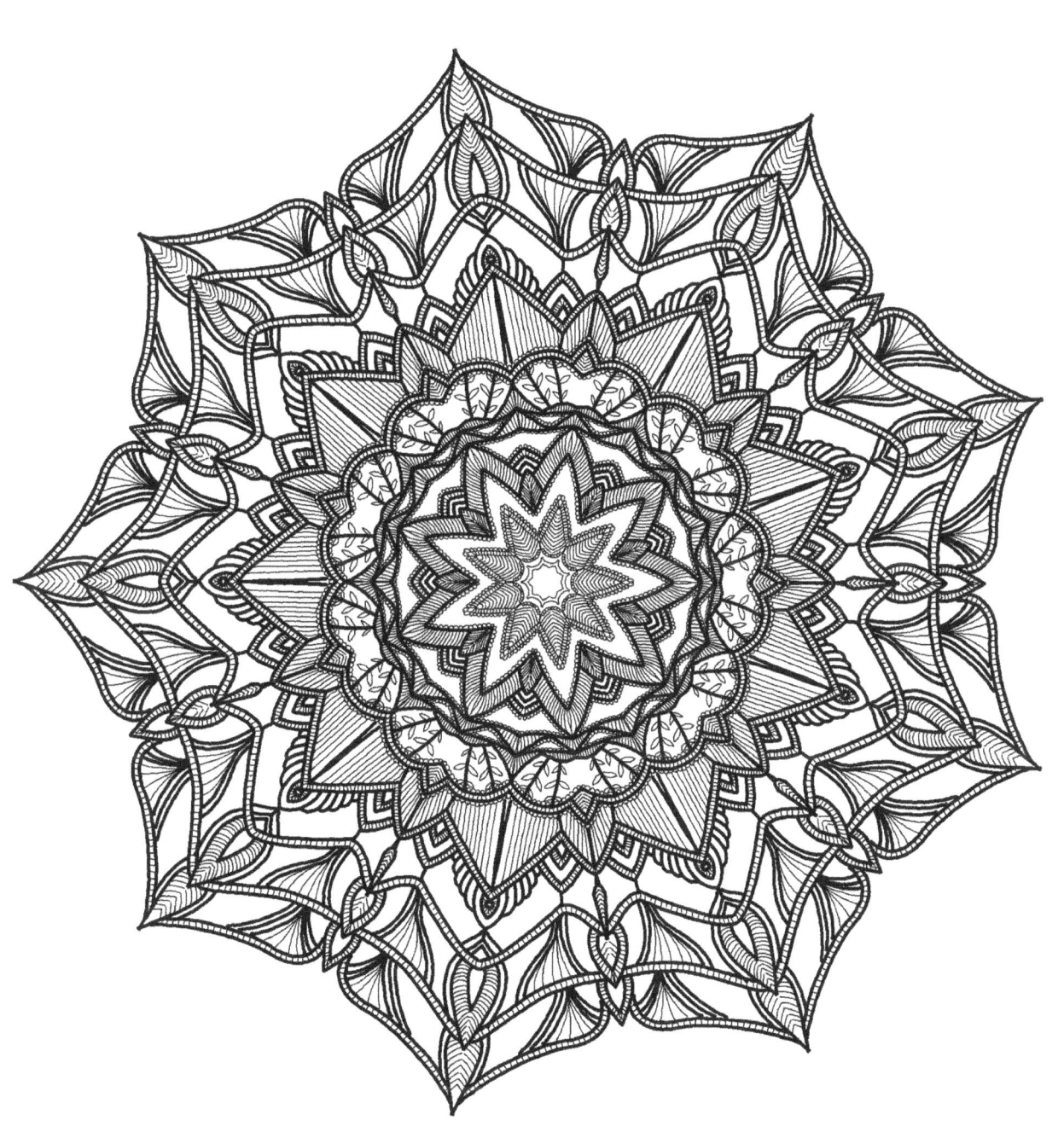

Keep Your Mind Open

www.ingramcontent.com/pod-product-compliance
Lightning Source LLC
Chambersburg PA
CBHW081201180526
45170CB00006B/2184